The Set Apart Way

for

Christ-Centered Creative Artists

A Practical Guide on How to Honor God with Your Gifts and Talents

Sepia Gladden

Publishing Style
Please note that in this work certain pronouns in Scripture that refer to the Father, Son, and Holy Spirit are capitalized and the name of satan and related names are not capitalized. We have chosen not to give satan any glory, whatsoever, even to the point of violating grammatical rules.

Published by:
Set Apart International Ministries
www.setapartinternationalministries.org
ISBN-13: 978-1-42764-558-6

Printed in the United States of America.
2010 First Edition

Edited by: Glenda Wright (Make It Plain Editing Service)
Cover Design by: Mytruebiz.com

TABLE OF CONTENTS

Based on the Word

The Scriptural foundation for this book is:

2 Timothy 2:20-22

"But in a great house there are not only vessels of gold and silver, but also of wood and clay, some for honor and some for dishonor. Therefore if anyone cleanses himself from the latter, he will be a vessel for honor, sanctified and useful for the Master, prepared for every good work."

Dedication

This book is dedicated not only to the current generation but also to future generations.

Acknowledgements

First and foremost to You, Lord Jesus, I give all the glory, honor and praise. For I clearly understand that without You, there would be no me. And I thank you publicly for the courage and confidence to write this book. Though the devil tried to prevent me from ever being the author that I am, I praise Your name over the fact that it did not work because greater is You that is in me than he that is in the world. And for my breaking, molding, processing, pain and even that in which I thought was nothing but delay, I thank You.

To my husband, Anthony Gladden, thank you for allowing me to be all God has created me to be without any hindrance whatsoever. Your support and encouragement has been **remarkable**. What a husband you are! For truly it has been and is an honor to be able to co-labor with you in the gospel of Christ Jesus.

To my children Liberty, Glory, and Kabowd Gladden boy, do I thank you for the greater level of freedom and glory you three have helped to birth in my life! Mommy loves you, and it's my prayer that you also will do all you do for the glory of God giving praise to Him through Jesus Christ.

India and Darryl Hines (mom and pops) Henry Stewart (Dad) Grandma and Grandpa Howard thanks for helping to protect, nurture, and guide me along the way until **finally** I came to meet Jesus, Who is the way, the truth, and the life. Thank you also for your tremendous support with this project. To my little bro, Clark, thank you for always encouraging me and telling me how proud you were of me even when you may not have always understood me. Max, DJ, and sisters, I love you all greatly and pray I am being a good example to follow.

To my mentors, pastors, leaders, elders, prophets, teachers, bishops, friends, etc. and to all who have ever had a part in my "making", truly, I thank you for being used by God to help me become all that I am today. May God continue to bless you exceedingly and abundantly with the greatest gift ever . . . being able to know Him in a more intimate way.

My Testimony

Like a light bulb coming on one day while I was writing this book, it occurred to me that before I can take you forward and share with you the revelation God has given to me about *The Set Apart Way for Christ-Centered Creative Artists*, I first needed to share with you my history. Out of obedience, I will now do just that. Being a Creative Artist in the world for many years and using my talents in a way that did not glorify God whatsoever and then coming into the Kingdom of God with a command to use my talents to glorify Him, I was faced with a huge challenge. This challenge existed because at the time, I had absolutely no idea how to make the change; however, one thing I did know was that if what I was going to be doing did not give God glory, then I did not want to be a part of it in any way. I had sensed God's hand upon my life so strongly, but I often wondered why others around me did not. Yet, I knew I had no choice except to yield to God's call and either do whatever I did for His glory or not at all.

I will never forget the first time I experienced a life-changing moment in my understanding of who God wanted me to be. It all happened when I attended a small church service and heard the preacher say if there was anything that was standing in the way of my relationship with God, then I needed to let it go. Immediately I knew what that one thing was and from that time on, I purposed in my heart to no longer allow my music and lyrics to be my god, but instead to trust **God** solely and submit to His will and purpose for my life. After that experience, I wholeheartedly threw myself into my relationship with God by letting Him know He was the one I wanted, not the fame, not the name, not the trinkets, nor the hype, but Him, and Him alone! When I did that, God allowed mentors to come my way and show me how I could go about using my gifts and talents for *His* glory. In submitting to God, I finally received the true and authentic peace I had been in constant pursuit of, not to mention, knowing that my talent was now being used to please God instead of only offending Him.

Yet, I later realized that what the Lord had allowed me to gain, I was responsible for sharing with others because as the word of God tells us, "to whom much is given much is required." Thus, out of obedience and a strong desire to see God's Shekinah glory restored back into the Creative Arts Ministry, I yielded to the Spirit of God and wrote this book.

A Word of Welcome

Because you picked up this book to read, it automatically tells me a couple of wonderful things about you. First and foremost, you have a strong desire to give God all the glory while using the gifts and talents He's given you. Second, you also have a teachable spirit, and both of these things in God's eyes, as well mine, are absolutely phenomenal! Indeed, this book was written to reveal different and practical things that we, as Creative Artists, can do in order to be transformed into "set apart", Christ-Centered, Creative Artists and vessels, for God's glory. In reading this book, you will see how I repeatedly use the word "we" instead of "you", and I did so on purpose that I may clearly point out the fact that I, myself, have not yet "arrived". I am continually yielding myself unto God so I will eventually be transformed more and more into His image.

Writing this book has truly been a journey for me . . . one in which I continue to learn from every time I read it. And it's my prayer that as you read it, you also will literally be able to see your walk with God being ushered into a greater level of intimacy while either learning or confirming what it takes to give God the glory by using the gifts and talents He has given you.

In this book, I have intentionally set out to encourage you, inspire you, confirm much of what you already know, and shed light upon that which you may not know. This book was the *action* I decided to take as a way to be a part of the solution instead of the problem. And by serving many years with many different Creative Artists, God has allowed me to gain quite a bit of wisdom as a result of seeing much of the good, bad, and ugly in the vessels chosen as Creative Artists. Some things I will intentionally share with you in this book, but solely for the purpose of pointing out different ways both you and I can use our gifts and talents for God's glory.

Tools you will need in order to effectively get the most from this book are:

#1 A heart opened to receive
#2 Time devoted to reading
#3 A Bible (The versions I chose to use the most are the New King James Version, as well as the Amplified Bible, and on occasion I used the New International Version of the Bible.)

A Message to the Seasoned Creative Artist

Proverbs 19:8 tells us, *"He who gets wisdom loves his own soul; and he who cherishes understanding prospers."* (NIV) Therefore, for you, who have already been using your gifts and talents for God's glory for quite a while and have gained much wisdom from your own personal experiences, I'd like to encourage you to share with others the lessons you've learned. I'd also like to thank you in advance for your humility in purposing to read this book.

For you, this book will be like going to the doctor's office to get a physical checkup just to make sure everything is still operating the way it should. However, if something should be detected that is hindering you from obtaining optimal health in your relationship with Christ, please know He welcomes you to get whatever it is you need from Him, while in the Great Physician's office. He desires for you to return to dynamic health and continue to be effective. Yet, for those of you who already know you will come out with an excellent report, I believe by reading this book, you will receive strength from the confirmations you'll receive. You will, in addition, receive strength to keep on representing Christ to the fullest.

Therefore, despite wherever you are in your walk with Christ, I implore you to take this journey with me by reading this work. Once you've finished, please either pass it along or simply bless another by purchasing another copy. That way, prayerfully, we as Creative Artists can collectively unite and be on one accord working toward the goal of being set apart, Christ-Centered Creative Artists as we represent Jesus to the world.

With warmest regards,

Sepia

PREFACE

What is The Set Apart Way?

The "set apart" way is the **straight and narrow path** God is calling all of His creative artists \ ministers to (Matthew 7:14). Because of this call, this book will literally break down many different principles on how you can use your gifts and talents in a set apart way for God's glory.

This book emphasizes the truth and that truth is that there truly is a set apart way God desires all of His Creative/Worship Arts Ministers to walk in so as a result we may be the salt of the earth and light that blazes in the midst of a world that is so desperately in need of knowing Jesus as their personal Lord and Savior.

This book will equip you with the following:

- **Truth** by exposing the difference between using your gifts and talents for God's glory versus using them for your flesh, the world, or the devil's glory.

- **Tools of support** by providing scriptural based wisdom throughout the book in order to encourage the set apart lifestyle.

- **Nuggets of practical application** by providing suggestions on what you can do in order to implement the suggested material in your life covered throughout this book in the section entitled "Walk It Out and Focus Questions" found at the end of every chapter.

- **Encouragement, empowerment, and strength** for the Set Apart Journey by closing out each chapter with a brief prayer under the "Let's Agree in Prayer" section.

- **Transparency** as a result of Sepia sharing many of her own personal experiences.

This book has been enhanced for individual or group study, and there is also a workbook that corresponds with this book entitled *"The Set Apart Way for Christ-Centered Creative Artists Bible Study Workbook."*

Chapter 1: Okay, God's Called You: Now What?

Position Yourself to Receive the Wisdom of God

After receiving our call in Christ, many times we are filled with so much passion and zeal that we want to take off running full speed ahead with our assignments. And this is perfectly understandable especially after you may have gone through years and years of wandering, going to and fro not knowing your purpose in life. However, the problem with just taking off running full speed is that many of us are only receiving the call but have yet to receive the needed instructions to go along with that call. It's true; some of us are getting so fired up that we're going and doing without first having the wisdom of God to know how to execute our assignments effectively. Wisdom 101 is a pre-requisite, and the major courses that follow are never-ending when seeking to effectively fulfill the call of God on our lives. Proverbs 19:2 (AMP) tells us, *"Desire without knowledge is not good, and to be overhasty is to sin and miss the mark,"* we must take heed and keep our enthusiasm to move forward too quickly in check.

So, if you already know you've been called by God, and have come into an understanding that God desires to use you to accomplish something great for His glory, you have every right to go ahead and celebrate the call, but then you must position yourself to receive the wisdom and Godly guidance that goes along with that call. Because, if our excitement is not channeled correctly, we can actually do more harm than good. This is how in the past Christians have made God's name look bad.

Proverbs 4:7 tells us: *"Wisdom is the principal thing; therefore get wisdom. And in all your getting, get understanding."*

> **Without having the wisdom of God, you will only shoot amiss allowing zeal to override getting the proper training needed to effectively fulfill the call.**

See the truth is if we don't have the wisdom of God with our assignment, we'll only shoot amiss with misdirected zeal and will not be able to hit the bull's eye. Yes, some instructions will only be given to us once we go and actually move into the assignment; yet it is still in our best interest to get as much information about the assignment beforehand as possible.

When we look at God's record, He revealed His perfect will to Moses pertaining to the freedom of the Israelites and building of His tabernacle. With Noah, He did the same with the instructions for building the ark, and we could cite many others in His word, to whom He revealed His vision of destiny and purpose. And because He is not a respecter of persons, He will do the same for us! All we have to do is simply ask, believe he'll answer, and position ourselves to receive it.

James 1:5 says: *"If any of you lacks wisdom, let him ask of God, who gives to all liberally and without reproach, and it will be given to him."*

Here are a few other biblical examples of those who had to receive more than just the call. David is one person because although he was anointed to be king, he first had to serve a king with humility and excellence before being released into his own kingship. Also the disciples because before they became apostles, they first had to be servants trained and taught by Jesus as He led by example. And it wasn't until Jesus knew the disciples were ready that He entrusted them to have the power needed to heal the sick, cast out demons, and preach the Kingdom of God (see Luke 9:1-2).

Now the question I have for us, Creative Artists, is who have we sat under to be taught? Who has approved us? Do we have power or only a heart's desire to help? Are we led by our emotions alone, meaning can we see the problems but not bring about any solutions and ultimately help others realize that deliverance comes only through Christ? I merely ask this because if we're not seeing ourselves operate in any kind of power, wouldn't have a clue what to do should a demon need to be cast out, don't have the faith to be used by God in order to heal the sick, or know how to lead sinners to Christ, etc., then I'd strongly recommend we pump our brakes, humble ourselves, and ask God to send us some of His generals in order to train us in these needed areas. Trust me! There has already been way too many who've charged off on the call alone and because of a lack of wisdom, humility, service, they only ended up getting burned out and/or "jacked up" by the devil. This is why we should never attempt to go out and make the call happen in our own strength because if we do, the outcome may be disastrous.

In fact, since wisdom is such a necessity to accompany our call, I'd like for us to take an in-depth look at what Proverbs 2:1-11 has to tell us about wisdom. It reads:

> *1 "My son, if you receive my words,*
> *And treasure my commands within you,*
> *2 So that you incline your ear to wisdom,*
> *And apply your heart to understanding;*
> *3 Yes, if you cry out for discernment,*
> *And lift up your voice for understanding,*
> *4 If you seek her as silver,*
> *And search for her as for hidden treasures;*
> *5 Then you will understand the fear of the LORD,*
> *And find the knowledge of God.*
> ***6 For the LORD gives wisdom;***
> ***From His mouth come knowledge and understanding;***
> *7 He stores up sound wisdom for the upright;*
> *He is a shield to those who walk uprightly;*
> *8 He guards the paths of justice,*
> *And preserves the way of His saints.*
> *9 Then you will understand righteousness and justice,*
> *Equity and every good path.*
> *10 When wisdom enters your heart,*
> *And knowledge is pleasant to your soul,*
> *11 Discretion will preserve you;*
> *Understanding will keep you."*

As you can see from what we read, wisdom is a very critical component of fulfilling our call. To obtain it, ask God for the "who, what, when, where, why, and how" then position yourself to hear and see exactly what God will say or do.

Luke 11:9 reads: *"So I say to you, **ask**, and it will be given to you; **seek**, and you will find; **knock** and it will be opened to you."*

Another profitable thing you can do in order to receive God's wisdom for your call is to connect with and serve those who operate in the same areas in which God is calling you. This doesn't necessarily mean you'll operate in your gifts and talents at that time, but you may do what the disciples did while walking with Jesus: serve and observe. So when it is your time to be released fully into your call, you can operate out of the wisdom of God instead of ignorance.

Proverbs 11:14 tells us: *"Where there is no counsel, the people fall; but in the multitude of counselors there is safety."*

Walk It Out and Focus Questions

➢ Prayer, fasting, humility, and getting away from all busyness to quiet your spirit man are definitely important things you can do in order to position yourself to receive the wisdom of God related to your call.

➢ If you don't already have a teachable spirit, please learn to develop one because this will make God and others eager to give you whatever it is you need in order to fulfill your call.

➢ Exodus 2:11-15 tells us about a situation where there was one who moved out of zeal but not out of wisdom. Who is this biblical example? What did he do? What was the result of what he did?

➢ Think back, do you recall any times when you moved out of zeal and not wisdom? If so, what were the results, and what could you have done differently?

➢ I'd like to encourage you to do a mini wisdom study by looking in a concordance or going to biblegateway.com to locate different scriptures where the term "wisdom" is used. The purpose of this activity is to learn something you didn't know about wisdom.

Let's Agree in Prayer: *Father, I thank you for choosing me to assist with Your will being done here on earth as it is in heaven, and now that I know I've been called, please help me to become a lover of Your wisdom so I may be guided according to Your will and not my will or the will of others. In Jesus' name I pray. Amen.*

Chapter 2: There Is a Wilderness!

Embrace Your Process

Rappers, singers, dancers, actors, writers, and other creative artists and everybody who desires to be used by God in His Kingdom know there is a wilderness you must walk through. Truly, there is no way around God's training process for our lives. This training is what I like to call "the wilderness".

The wilderness is a time of preparation, a time where we learn God's ways through God's word. It's a time to read the scriptures, but most importantly, it's a time to learn how to live out and walk out those scriptures. It is a time where we, as artists, must come to accept the fact that we do need to be trained and have our minds renewed so we can know God's will, especially since many of us have only known the ways of the world. So, the wilderness is a place where we can begin to learn how to spend more time with God instead of being all wrapped up in the things of this world. We must do exactly what Matthew 6:33 has exhorted us to do: "*Seek ye first the Kingdom of God and His righteousness . . .*"

When in the wilderness, you may also feel led to spend more time with God than even the amount of time you spend working on and developing your gifts and talents. I say this because sometimes, whether knowingly or unknowingly, we spend more time trying to perfect our gifts and talents than we spend with the One who gave them to us, God. So the wilderness will teach us how to trust Him in a greater way and know He's the One who gives us whatever we need, whenever it's needed. Many great revelations will come forth when we deliberately choose to devote the time we could've taken for ourselves and our skills and instead use it to focus solely on Him. The truth of the matter is that we spend "hour after hour" in preparation, when God can give us what we need in the blink of an eye.

Where you are in your walk with Christ will determine what takes place during your wilderness experiences.

The wilderness, too, is a time of reflection where we should seriously pay close attention to everything God shows us that does not line up with His will, so with His help, prayerfully, we can eliminate those things. Normally when we are in the wilderness, it may cause us to be separated from our families, friends, associates, and possibly even a few church members. Why? It's when we're all alone that the Lord can have our undivided attention and pour into us from His Spirit and we can learn to minister to Him also.

Not to mention, if you're truly being led by the Holy Spirit, this time can also cause you to be separated from certain types of entertainment like music, TV, movies, etc. or basically from any and everything that does not feed your spirit man in a way that promotes your growth in Christ. The wilderness is a time of character building: a time where you learn to reverence the Lord in a more devoted way.

In addition, you might even go through classroom training to further your education about Christ while in the wilderness. I know some great classes I'd recommend are ones where you can learn more about other religions so you can be exposed to different cultures and the reasons why they do certain things.

I'd also recommend you take a class on spiritual warfare so you can learn not only about the tactics of your enemy, satan, but also learn about the enemies that may live within you.

Where you are in your walk with Christ is what will actually determine what will or will not take place during your times in the wilderness. And notice I said times being plural and not singular. I said this because even Jesus, our example, had many times where He, Himself, had to go to a place of solitude with God; He had wilderness experiences. As a matter of fact, for all who've been or will be used by God, it's a guarantee they also have either had them or will have them. This is why it's really best for all of us to expect them, accept them, and learn everything we can while in them because believe me, once we come out, it's then test time. It's time to apply all we've learned.

I know when I first received the call of God to be a minister, God separated me from my immediate family, church, job, and even the state where I lived and sent me right back to my original birth place which happened to be 500 miles away. In that particular wilderness experience, God led me to a small church where I could become more intimate with Him. And looking back, I can really say that was a phenomenal experience. Of course, it didn't always feel phenomenal when I was directly in the midst of it, if you know what I mean.

Although I was only in that wilderness for six months, at the time, it still felt like an eternity because I thought God was going to make me stay there forever. However, God later advised I could leave. And when I finally returned to Atlanta, I was in a whole different kind of wilderness, one I'd like to categorize as being intense boot camp training because this time I was required to learn extensively. I learned from things like my New Member's classes which covered baptism, salvation, tithing, and a lot of other foundational things in Christ. These classes took four months to complete. Then I joined an evangelism ministry to serve my local church with my gifts and talents and that training took two months. I also took a class on spiritual warfare which took three months, and a class on the great truths of the bible which took a year. Following that, I took a class on cult awareness which took two months. The next class I took was "Walking in Deliverance" to gain an understanding of what I and others needed deliverance from, and that took three months. Then by God's divine orchestration, I was placed in the Minister's in Training program at my church, which required a much greater level of preparation. I could go on and on, but I just wanted to share a few of my own personal wilderness experiences so you could see how they may differ from time to time and from person to person.

But in essence, regardless of what your wilderness may be, I'd like to strongly encourage you to yield to it and not resist it because whether you want to or not, at God's appointed time, wilderness experiences will be required. I can tell you from experience that it's much better to go through it with God in His timing, opposed to having to come back later and do it out of desperation. Therefore, as I stated in the subtitle of this chapter, embrace your wilderness process even though it may be painful in one way or another. Be assured, it is well worth it in the long run.

Walk It Out and Focus Questions

> ➤ When "placed in the wilderness," ask God to help you appreciate it and not despise, complain, resist or discredit it.
> ➤ Allow nothing or no one to rush your process with God, and when you're directly in the midst of it, stand on knowing that God is aligning everything according to His perfected order for your life. Please read (Romans 8:28).

➤ While in the wilderness if you're tempted to abort it for some reason, declare and stand on this truth for strength, "That **all things** shall be added unto you after you have first sought the Kingdom of God and His righteousness." (Matthew 6:33)

➤ Keep your eyes stayed upon God at all times; never look to the left or to the right, meaning try not to compare your wilderness with the wilderness of others, since we all have different journeys to travel with God.

➤ The wilderness is a great place for God to deal with any areas of our lives which would hinder us from walking in His holiness and prevent His will from being accomplished in and through us. Surrender your all to Him so that whatever you need will be addressed.

➤ When Moses was in his wilderness, (Please read Exodus 3 and Exodus 4.), what were some of the things Moses told God he struggled with, and what did God do in order to assist Moses with his struggles?

Let's Agree in Prayer: *Father since Psalm 127:1 says: "Unless the LORD builds the house, they labor in vain who build it…" please help me to allow only You to build my house by accepting whatever and whenever my times of wilderness may occur. In Jesus' name I pray. Amen.*

Chapter 3: No Word, No Ministry

Are You Equipped?

If we don't know the word of God, meaning the Holy Spirit inspired and Spirit-breathed word of the Bible, then we're not yet qualified to do effective ministry. Why? The answer to that question is simple because not knowing the word of God means we're not fully clothed in our armor; we don't know how to use what God has already given us as our weaponry, and we can only impart to people from our flesh instead of God and His pure, unadulterated word. However, not being qualified is something that *can* change; this is why I said, not **yet** qualified.

When you think about civilians who enlist in the army wanting to become soldiers, the first thing they have to do is go through training and learn how to suit up in their armor but also how to effectively use their weapons. It's not until they've proven to their sergeant that they know what they're doing that they can be released to go to war. An untrained, unarmed soldier is not only in danger but also dangerous.

If you do not know the word of God, then you are not yet qualified to do effective ministry.

If you're asking yourself, "How in the world do armor, war, and training all tie into knowing the word of God?" let me explain. The moment we accepted Jesus as being our personal Lord and Savior, we entered into a war, a war where satan constantly fights against everything that's of God including the children (sons) of God; that's you and me. (Please read Revelation 12:17.) So, we are required to fight whether we want to or not. This is why we've been encouraged in Ephesians 6:11 from the Amplified Bible to: "*Put on God's **whole armor** [the armor of a heavy-armed soldier which God supplies], that you may be able successfully to stand up against [all] the strategies and the **deceits** of the devil.*"

The armor Ephesians 6:14-18 outlines is essential to those on the frontlines and even those bringing up the rear. In fact, Ephesians 6:17 tells us that part of our armor is the sword of the Spirit, which is the word of God. This is something we've all been thoroughly encouraged and admonished to "take up" since certainly the attacks will come. Now, when I speak of "wearing your armor," I mean being equipped with and fully versed in specific scriptures we may use as a defense or even offense concerning every battle in which we may find ourselves engaged. This explains the reason why boot camp is a necessity and not an option; it is to be taken extremely serious and not bypassed because if it is bypassed, the blood will be on our hands alone. Remember your life and the lives of others will be affected by how well you are trained and equipped. And a good "soldier" cannot wait until the battle begins before being trained.

Ephesians 6:12 from the Amplified Bible tell us: "*We are not wrestling with flesh and blood [contending only with physical opponents], but against the despotisms, against the powers, against [the master spirits who are] the world rulers of this present darkness, against the spirit forces of wickedness in the heavenly (supernatural) sphere.*" We're told by this scripture not only are we contending with things in the natural but also things in the spirit realm. This is why it's a must (I said a MUST.) that we pray for greater discernment and know the word of God so we will be able to defeat our enemy, satan.

By the way, we can also become aware of the true necessity of knowing the word of God by reading Matthew 4:1-11. These verses illustrate how Jesus actually defeated satan by simply using the word of God. If Jesus hadn't been equipped with the word (His sword), He could've been defeated, and this also holds true for those of us who are not equipped with the word.

Hebrews 4:12 tells us: "*For the word of God is living and powerful, and sharper than any two-edged sword, piercing even to the division of soul and spirit, and of joints and marrow, and is a discerner of the thoughts and intents of the heart.*"

Further, 2 Corinthians 10:3-4 from the Amplified Bible tells us: "*For though we walk (live) in the flesh, we are not carrying on our warfare according to the flesh and using mere human weapons. For the weapons of our warfare are not physical [weapons of flesh and blood], **but they are mighty** before God for the overthrow and destruction of strongholds.*"

Did you know that satan even knows the power of God's word? Well it's true! He is quite aware of its potency and that is primarily why his main objective is trying to keep us so busy with any and everything that we don't have time to read, study or understand the word of God. Distraction is one of his greatest tactics to get and keep us off course. This is because he knows if we become skilled in applying the word of God in our lives, we will have an effective weapon against him. Recall 2 Corinthians 10:3-4 has told us we would be able to fight effectively using the word of God. This certainly explains why many times we have to fight so hard just to read and meditate on it. Selah. (Meaning, "stop and think about that.")

Since we do have to fight, I suggest that you become proactive against satan and flip the script on him. How? Start setting up appointments with God intentionally to spend time with Him and to purposely read His word like you'd schedule anything else you have to do. If you want to be effective and victorious these two things are vital. The word of God, itself, exhorts us to discipline ourselves in it: "*Study and be eager and do your utmost to present yourself to God approved (tested by trial), a workman who has no cause to be ashamed, correctly analyzing and accurately dividing [rightly handling and skillfully teaching] the word of truth.*" (2 Timothy 2:15 AMP)

I've briefly shared why we all need to know the word of God, I'll now share some of the ways I, in the past, disciplined myself to remember more of God's word. One thing I did for quite a while was I refused to allow myself to eat lunch until I first studied the word, and I stood on Deuteronomy 8:3 for strength and endurance which says: "*Man does not live by bread alone but by every word that proceeds out of the Lord's mouth.*"

I also took a job which allowed me to work while I listened to the word, so by God's grace I was able to "feed myself" the word for hours at a time while keying information into the computer. Before I continue, let me point out that, yes, there are jobs such as cleaning, data entry, customer service, and even jobs in the computer field etc., where you can . . . *believe it or not* get paid to work while sowing into your spirit at the same time. How? Mainly, because some companies do not care what you listen to as long as you get the job done. Talk about being motivated to work!

However, if a job switch is not an option for you, and you can't listen to anything while you work or have a micromanager, you can still try this: I wrote the word of God down on flash cards so whenever I went to the bathroom, took breaks, or ate lunch, etc., I could study them. Because I looked for doors of opportunity to study God's word, He opened them so not only could I meditate and study it but also test myself for accountability. Interestingly enough, I still have many of those same flash cards all over my house and car which I still review in order to show myself approved unto God.

Seriously, if you have not already begun to study, learn and understand the word of God in a very intimate way, please do so! Not only will you become qualified to effectively minister but most importantly, you'll be able to know God in a more intimate way and survive attacks from the enemy fighting every battle effectively using the word and by the grace of God. Know that it's our level of retaining and understanding the word that increases our ability to "work the word" and that also determines whether we will or will not be victorious in this war we are in. Please do not take what I said lightly.

Walk It Out and Focus Questions

> Think of several different realistic ways in which you can go about remembering more of God's word. Then after you discover those ways, commit to practicing them and tell someone else so they can help hold you accountable.
> In your attempts to retain more of God's word within you, I'd like to suggest that you work your way up. Take small steps so you don't get overwhelmed, and if for any reason you get off track with it, never give up! Just pick up where you left off and keep going.
> 2 Timothy 3:15-17 tells us about many benefits of knowing the word of God. What are they? Can you locate any other scriptures that also explain the benefits of knowing the word of God?

Let's Agree in Prayer: *Lord, please help me to become a skilled, disciplined warrior in Your word, so ultimately I may be wise in all that I do for You as well as be protected from the schemes of the devil. In Jesus' name I pray. Amen.*

Chapter 4: Know Your History

Your Past Plays a Vital Part in Your Future

I heard someone ask, "How can you truly go forward without first knowing your history?" Since I've been able to see the truth in this somewhat simple question, I wholeheartedly agree with the need to examine and answer it. It really is important for us to take the time to find out about our history and heritage especially as it relates to our new adoptive family in Christ.

Ephesians 1:5 in the Amplified Bible tells us: "*For He foreordained us (destined us, planned in love for us) to be adopted (revealed) as His own children through Jesus Christ, in accordance with the purpose of His will [because it pleased Him and was His kind intent].*"

After I discovered that some of us do not know much about our history in Christ, to the point of not knowing much about the old covenant and/or why there was even a need for the new covenant, or about Israel being God's chosen nation, along with any of their customs or history, I decided to bring up this topic. If you're a child of God, it is not only the Israelites' history but also your history. So I wrote this chapter in hopes of provoking all of us to either begin to dig into our history or go deeper than where our understanding currently is. We need to know a lot more about our history besides the fact that Jesus died on the cross for our sins. Although Jesus' death on the cross for our sins and His resurrection are the keys to our salvation, there is so much more to gain by understanding our bloodline in Christ. And I believe after you've been in the faith for a while, it's time for you to step into the deeper things of God, that you continue to show yourself approved unto God.

> **The time has come for us not only to focus on our own personal testimonies but also to balance it with God's history.**

You see, I believe the time has come for us not only to focus on our own personal testimonies but also to balance them with God's history so we are able to elaborate on and teach others about God's recorded divinity, love, justice, wrath, purposes, attributes, etc. Another important factor to mention as we study our history is that we will discover certain patterns that illustrate that God is the same God yesterday, today, and forevermore (Hebrews 13:8).

As we become more informed about our history, we will be able to reach out to and fellowship with a more diverse group of people because as you may or may not know, some religions are more knowledgeable about our history than even we are. And to that they laugh. Yes, many have become deaf and unresponsive to our faith primarily because they think we're ignorant; however, even though we will never be able to learn everything about God because of His vastness, I know it'll speak volumes to God, ourselves, and others if we're at least in continual pursuit of knowledge of Him and His greatness.

As it was once told to me, I'd like to also recommend to you that Christians should always make the extra effort to stay in a posture of continuous learning about God. We should always maintain a teachable spirit especially since there's so much to learn about the God who created the universe and everything in it. One great way to do that is to attend regular, intimate bible classes in order to help further your growth in Christ.

In fact, many churches nowadays have such a desire to help educate and equip the Body of Christ they are making many resources available to do so. Some churches have their classes set up like a bible school where the only cost to attend is your time. If this is something you'd be interested in, consider calling different churches in your community to see whether they have classes, and if so and you are led by the Holy Spirit, (ensuring that they are providing sound teaching) register and attend. You'll see your growth in Christ go to a whole new level.

In addition to learning more about your history in Christ, I'd like to also encourage you to learn more about your biological family because I believe there's a wealth of liberating information stored up for you to receive if only you'd seek it out. Although I realize everybody's past contains different degrees of pain, I also know with God's strength He can work wonders and perform miracles in helping us face whatever we need in order to be supernaturally equipped and free as He would have us to be.

Before you begin your "searching out process," I suggest you ask God to cover your emotions before, during, and after seeking out information so you're not affected or hindered by what you discover. Also ask God to open doors of opportunity where your family will be willing to share their history with you because trust me, many folks do not like to talk about their pasts. However, since you know it's imperative for your future, don't give up. Keep searching! I pray whatever God allows you to discover will only bring forth and result in what is needed to propel you further into your destiny.

I know when I first set out to dig deeper into my family's history, I learned quite a bit about the generational curses in it, ones that could've had a horrible effect on me had it not been for the blood of Jesus and being at least partially aware of my history. After finding out many things, I was then able to address whatever tried to rise up against me instead of accepting it or ignore it. By knowing more about my history, I am no longer ignorant to many of the things I once merely asked "Wow! Where in the world did that come from?" Now I know.

The few reasons I just listed should make it vitally clear that your biological history is important; therefore, I encourage you as I encourage myself to learn more about our natural history and the family in Christ into which we've been adopted. Prayerfully, it will help us to flourish in every area of our lives.

Walk It Out and Focus Questions

> ➢ To become more knowledgeable about your history in Christ, the bible is certainly the greatest place to start. After all, it is a whole book of God's recorded history.
> ➢ Seek out classes, books, magazines, movies, websites, etc. that contain more in-depth information about Israel since you may not always hear about it frequently or be taught this much needed data in local congregations.
> ➢ Look up the meaning to some of the customs and feasts of the Israelites because this also will be helpful information to know. You can find this by looking at references right in the bible or checking a bible dictionary.

➢ Do you know what the old covenant and new covenant are and why there was a need for the new covenant? If not, by learning the answers to these questions you will understand more about your history.

Let's Agree in Prayer: *Father, please place an inquisitive and teachable spirit within me as it pertains to knowing more about my history so I never become stagnant or even comfortable in what I already know. And please lead me to all the tools I need so that I may grow in knowledge, wisdom and in understanding through these resources and endeavors. In Jesus' name I pray. Amen.*

Chapter 5: Know Your Differences and Embrace Them

Your Uniqueness Is Necessary

Because we all represent different parts within the Body of Christ, in this chapter I truly want to emphasize and help you learn to accept your uniqueness in Him. Though we've all been given the same commission found in Matthew 28:19-20, we've also all been gifted in many different ways to effectively fulfill that commission. 1 Corinthians 12:4-6 tells us: "*There are diversities of gifts, but the same Spirit. There are differences of ministries, but the same Lord. And there are diversities of activities, **but it is the same God who works all in all**.*"

Let's read what 1 Corinthians 12:18-19 also tells us. It reads: "*But now God has set the members, each one of them, in the body just as He pleased. And if they were all one member, where would the body be?*" I love the way verse 19 encourages us to be unique.

While on this journey with God, one of the things we must know is that just as no one else on the face of this earth has the same fingerprints, there also is no one else packaged in the exact same way we each have been created by God. For indeed, God has molded, formed and fashioned each and every one of us in a very unique, matchless, one of a kind, exceptional, and distinctive way. And our past experiences, circumstances, environments, and even families have all contributed to this uniqueness.

> **When you are only a God pleaser you can then truly appreciate your individuality in Christ Jesus.**

If for some reason you have not yet been able to identify your uniqueness in Christ, one thing you can do to discover it is to continue spending more and more time with the heavenly Father. I'm here to assure you that as you focus on Him, in His timing He will allow you to focus on the uniqueness and greatness of His character that lives inside of you by revealing it through His Holy Spirit or divine connections. That is the key required to unmask and unlock the real you. Another thing that will help you identify your uniqueness in God is making sure that you are only a "God pleaser". When you are, it will enable you to appreciate your individuality in Christ instead of becoming stuck in the bondage of attempting to be what others want you to be, or being another copycat, that is. Also, when you're not a "people pleaser," you can begin to walk in a greater level of confidence knowing there is a specific, amazing reason why God has allowed you to do what you do, the way that only you do it.

Prime example, when I first started using my gifts and talents for God, I was a little disappointed because I couldn't understand why the music I created was not the kind of music to really "move" a crowd. Eventually I came to understand that the call on my life was to impart by teaching and preaching. As a result of that, I found out whether I rapped, did spoken word, poetry, or wrote, etc., the teaching gift would come forth in that specific form so I no longer worried about whether I moved a crowd or not.

Yet, while in the process of discovering more about the special creation that I am, I also came to understand that there's a need for teaching, preaching, deliverance, etc. through music. There's also truly a need for the type of music that will "just move a crowd", get folks "crunk" and "hyped" for Christ. Let me explain why I say that. Honestly, some of us are waaaaaaaaay too serious at times, so we need different avenues to have fun and experience greater levels of freedom in Christ and the joy that comes from knowing Him. Again, this is why it's very beneficial to know what your differences in Christ are so you can be effective.

Allow me to share another example with you. When I first read this chapter to my husband, who is also a poet, he told me he could honestly relate to what I was saying because one thing that often frustrated him when he first started doing poetry was recognizing that he did not have this certain type of "flow" or style that others had. Because of that, he wondered if he was really called to do poetry at all. He said it wasn't until he actually spent intimate time with the Lord that he came to know that his uniqueness in poetry called for him to do it in a theatrical way. Once he came to understand that, he realized his flow was precisely right for how God wanted to use his talent. After that revelation, he had much greater peace and was finally able to embrace his own uniqueness.

The reason I'm stressing this topic is because I believe wholeheartedly that many who may not fit into the "normal mode" of how things are usually done in the church or other venues have literally quenched and buried their uniqueness. As a word of encouragement to you, I'd like to bring to your attention that John the Baptist, Jesus, Paul and so many others throughout the bible did not fit into the norm, but praise God they embraced their uniqueness! Praise God! Nothing ever prevented them from being all that God had called them to be.

I can tell you up-front, just as God created us to be a very diverse group of people upon the earth, it's a guarantee we will not always be accepted by everyone we encounter. Nevertheless, for those who don't know how to quite receive our uniqueness, we have to be sure we still show these individuals the love of Christ. If it's the will of God for them to know more about us, in His timing, He will be the One who shows them the true need for our uniqueness and ministry.

Please understand, many of us have been called to make a very *radical* impact for Christ, and there will be times where, undoubtedly, we will be looked upon as being very strange and peculiar. The reason I'm writing this is to speak life into your spirit and to let you know that as long as you are not shaming the name of Christ, He embraces you. And guess what? IT IS ALL GOOD. ALL GOOD! Eventually your uniqueness will minister to the very ones who may have once questioned your individuality and differences or misunderstood you.

Again, please allow God to bring forth the unique character and gifts He has placed inside of you, so you can embrace them and also be able to display the vast creativity of God Almighty to this lost, hurt, and dying world. Whether you know this or not, there are those who are waiting for your uniqueness to come forth so they can finally have someone with whom they can identify. Yes, you must know that by being you, the destiny of so many others will be unlocked.

Walk It Out and Focus Questions

> ➢ Read and meditate often on 1 Corinthians 12 because it points out the different parts of the Body of Christ and how we all are needed for it to operate effectively.
> ➢ Intentionally identify your uniqueness in the Body of Christ by writing it down, and then write down why you feel or know your uniqueness in Christ is needed.
> ➢ How was John the Baptist and Jesus different? If you don't know, do a study on them. This will certainly encourage you to be YOU.
> ➢ Can you think of anyone in the Body of Christ who ministers in a very unique creative way? If so, who are they and how has their uniqueness been used to benefit the Kingdom of God?

Let's Agree in Prayer: *Father, for everything You have allowed to fashion me creatively, I thank you! Help me to forever appreciate my differences and know that everything You created is and will always be good. In Jesus' name I pray. Amen.*

Chapter 6: Your Gifts Will Make Room for You

Kill the Hustle and Allow God to Position You

We are told in Proverbs 18:16 that: *"A man's gift makes room for him, and brings him before great men."* I can't tell you how many times I've seen folks who've made room for their gifts opposed to allowing their gifts to make room for them the way Proverbs 18:16 says it should be. I mean I've watched some artists literally drain themselves to the point of no end by doing all types of things like trying to tell everybody about what all they can do, attending every event possible to meet and greet the "who's who" in the industry. Basically, if you name the "hustle", some have used it to promote themselves maybe in a "cleaner" version because it has to do with God.

Yet, what many in God's Kingdom have not discovered is that there's a huge difference (like night and day) between being successful in this world and being successful in the Kingdom of God. See when Christ is your primary focus, I'm here to tell you, God will allow you to be ushered into such a marvelous place in Him that you literally will no longer have to do what many in the Body are doing: spending all their money and time trying to market themselves almost on the verge of compromising, and running around exhausted trying to make it in this world in the "world's" way.

> **There's a huge difference (like night and day) between being successful in this world and being successful in the Kingdom of God.**

That's right! Instead of those things, God will grant you access to His peace and rest in place of the turmoil that comes from always trying to live up to what this world deems success. To be real with you, if you try to accomplish success the world's way, there are times you will have to get your hustle on. You might have to pound the pavement just to make it. You may possibly have to swing from the rafters to get man's attention or they are not going to pay you any attention. However, once you've put your total trust in God and not in your flesh and the world, your greatest deliverance will come from knowing you've made Jesus Lord over your life. Therefore, you've already achieved the highest level of success there is. Why? Jesus is the definition of success and **total** fulfillment, and that means "overflow".

In addition to what has already been discussed, the reason there are still quite a few artists who have become consumed with the fleshly mindset of attempting to make whatever it is they do for God happen on their own is because many do not totally trust their personal relationship with God. As a result of this, they do not trust Him to open doors for them supernaturally, without any involvement from them whatsoever. However, for those who feel this way, Philippians 4:6-7 tells us: *"Be anxious for nothing, but in everything by prayer and supplication, with thanksgiving, **let your requests be made known to God; and the peace of God**, which surpasses all understanding, **will guard your hearts and minds through Christ Jesus**."*

In fact, if Philippians 4:6-7 were to be applied on a much larger scale and on a deeper level guess what? We wouldn't see a lot of the hustle and bustle we witness taking place, but we'd see more artists walking in greater peace and confidence because of their dependence on Christ. Yes, the hustle would cease knowing whatever God has for them to do is exactly what will happen regardless of what anyone else tries to dictate.

And listen, when you receive this type of revelation . . . Boy, oh boy! It takes a whole lot of pressure off of you feeling the need to do this or that just to be seen, know this clique, or even be a part of this or that church to be known. If you ask me, those things are the same things the world does, and they discredit the authentic differences between success in God and worldly success.

One of my purposes for writing this chapter was to bring light to the truth; the truth is there is a huge difference! When you allow your gifts to make room for you while trusting in the One, who gave them to you, it's guaranteed you will witness the difference. Once you sit back, rest and watch God do what He's an expert at doing, orchestrating things to work on your behalf to accomplish His predestined will, you'll not only know and see the difference, but you'll also live the difference.

I'll demonstrate the true differences between when God opens a door and when man does it in their own strength by sharing one of my own experiences where I know it was nobody but God who opened this door for me.

I attended a church in Columbus, Ohio, and my pastor knew I rapped. Although he had never heard me, he told me one day he was going to allow me to do so. Yet, because so much time had passed since he'd made that statement, I really didn't think too much about it. But God . . .

It was New Year's Eve, one of the biggest service nights of the year. After standing in the freezing cold in a line wrapped clear around the church, I was eventually seated in the balcony. As I sat there praising God, suddenly my pastor started talking about a young person he knew who could rap, and he wanted them to come forward. So, as the whole church sat patiently waiting for this rapper to appear, so did I. I, too, was ready to see who this rapper was. To my surprise, my pastor was peering all the way through the crowd looking way up into the balcony my way, but since I had absolutely no clue who he was talking about, I also looked around. Finally, a friend nudged me and said, "Hey he's talking about you."

Once I realized he was talking about me, it felt like my heart stopped working! I remember saying to myself, "Oh my God, he really is talking about me!" Once I came out of shock mode, I mustered up the strength, even with all the butterflies fluttering in my stomach, and went down to the altar and was obedient to go forth in my ministry of rap. To God be all the glory! He surprisingly allowed me to minister that night before maybe a couple of thousand people, where a famous football player was one of the guest speakers seated on the front row. That was truly a night I will never forget.

I can honestly attest that God's awesomeness is responsible for every opportunity I've had to go forth and do what I do for God even though I only shared one experience. It really has been miraculous. The Encarta Dictionary defines miraculous as: 1) Regarded as caused by supernatural intervention (apparently contrary to the laws of nature and caused by a supernatural power) 2) Extraordinary (totally unexpected and marvelous).

Therefore, in essence, when it is God who has opened a door for you, it'll be something you'll most likely never forget. You will feel extreme gratitude towards God for what He has done knowing beyond a shadow of a doubt the credit cannot be given to you, your talent, or to anybody else. For it belongs to God and God alone.

Walk It Out and Focus Questions

> ➤ Look up the word <u>hustle</u> in a dictionary, and then ask yourself if the definition describes any of your actions? And if so, ask God to help you be transformed from being a hustler and only put your complete trust in Him.
> ➤ Whenever you see your flesh trying to make room for you instead of allowing God to do so, one thing you can do to stop this is to intentionally pull back from the situation. By doing this, it will force you to put your **total** trust in God *and* bring your flesh under submission to His will . . . for that matter.

Let's Agree in Prayer: *Father, please help me to be anxious for nothing but instead to trust You for everything knowing that You who have begun a good work in me shall complete it until the day of Jesus Christ (Philippians 1:6). And Father please help me to repeatedly, intentionally move out of the way so I may position myself to continually see You do the miraculous on my behalf. In Jesus' name I pray. Amen.*

Chapter 7: Humble Yourself!

Strip Yourself Just as Jesus Did

Humility was placed strongly in my spirit as a concept and principle in which I needed to expound upon because it is truly a prerequisite for using our gifts and talents in a "set apart way". I also was led to go into greater depth about being humble because pride is very blatant among some who call themselves Christian artists. I believe this exists because there is such a lack of true understanding about the severity and detestation of pride in God's eyes. And so because of this, I will attempt to shed some light on these topics in this chapter.

Unfortunately, possession of a proud spirit has almost become normal among Christians. Quite a few artists give very little thought to being prideful in their dealings with others and in the way they view themselves and gifts. Many do not know that God **absolutely hates pride**. Why? One of the main reasons is because it's the exact opposite of what He loves, humility.

However, humility is totally contrary to the world's way of doing and thinking about things. In this world, it is all about you and nobody else; it is all about what you can do, how well you can do it, how beautiful or handsome you look, what you have, and how skilled you are at this and that and on and on. This being the case, when you use your talents specifically for the world you do so in a way to intentionally lift yourself up and not the name of the Lord. This world's system is a self-centered and self-indulging system.

On the other hand, in God's Kingdom because He paid such a dear price for us . . . not with money but with the very blood of Jesus, His Son (1 Peter 1:18-19), our talents are no longer intended to be used for serving ourselves, and/or satan. They're meant to be used to serve God and bring Him glory and to collectively bless both His Body (the Body of Christ) and non-believers. James 4:10 tells us when we humble ourselves in the sight of the Lord, **HE** will lift us up.

Since pride is one of the most prominent characteristics of this world system, (See 1 John 2:15-16), there is a great need to break down the differences between pride versus humility. By doing this, we can honestly identify where we stand as it relates to walking in humility or pride. Let's take a quick glance at some of the differences between the two:

Pride
- Is of the world and satan
- It's all about me, myself, and I, and it's where you only look out for your self interests.
- You've put your trust in flesh, yourself and others.
- You desperately crave receiving praise from man.
- Puffed up, arrogant, haughty spirit
- Nobody can tell you anything because you already know everything.
- Your trust is in your talents and gifts.

Humility
- Is of God

- It's a lifestyle of servanthood where you constantly look out for the interest of others.
- You depend on God for everything.
- You only allow God and others to praise you opposed to you praising yourself (Proverbs 27:1) Note: We must also be very careful about how we receive and view the praise of man because the very ones who exalt us may be the ones to bring us down.
- You have a modest opinion of yourself.
- You have a teachable spirit, meaning you're open to receive correction, rebuke, wisdom, etc. because you know you are in need of help.
- Your trust is not in your talents or gifts but in God, the One who gave you the gifts and the ability to operate in them.

Before we move forward, take another look at the list of traits that go with pride and humility. Would you say your present heart condition is best described by the traits associated with pride or humility?

Jeremiah 17:9 tells us: "*The heart is deceitful above all things, and desperately wicked; who can know it?*" Perhaps you need to seek the Lord and receive revelation from Him about your heart condition and lifestyle. Because of this passage, we should never merely judge ourselves by our own hearts because of its wicked state, but instead judge ourselves according to the word of God and the fruit we display. By being an artist, myself, I'm here to tell you I know how easy it can be for pride to creep in and overtake us especially if we're not extremely cautious. By doing continual self checks on our spirit man, as well as, doing things to intentionally humble ourselves as Jesus, our example, did we can turn a characteristic that God hates into something that pleases Him, with his help, of course.

In God's Kingdom you will either humble yourself or be humbled, You will either fall on the rock to be broken or the rock will fall on you.

As a matter of fact as a way to share greater insight into the reasons God hates pride and encourages humility, I compiled another list of the scriptures found in God's word. Let's take a look at the following:

With Pride
- There will be shame and emptiness. (Proverbs 11:2)
- You will have strife. (Proverbs 13:10)
- Soon to fall and be destroyed (Proverbs 16:18)
- Known from afar (Psalm 138:6)
- You will be brought low. (Proverbs 29:23 and Psalm 147:6)
- You will be an enemy of God. (Proverbs 8:13)

With Humility
- You will have wisdom. (Proverbs 11:2)
- You will retain honor. (Proverbs 29:23)
- God will save you. (2 Samuel 22:28)
- God will not forget your cry. (Psalm 9:12)
- God will guide you in justice. (Psalm 25:9)
- God will beautify you with salvation. (Psalm 149:4)

- God will lift you up. (Psalm 147:6)
- God will keep you with His grace. (Proverbs 3:34)
- God will dwell with you and revive your spirit and heart. (Isaiah 57:15)
- You will inherit the earth and have an abundance of peace. (Psalm 37:11 and Matthew 5:5)

Even looking at this short list of scriptures, I think all would agree that taking the path of humility is a much more beneficial way of living than walking in pride. In fact, if the truth is really told, in God's Kingdom you will either humble yourself with God's grace or be humbled. You will either let yourself intentionally fall upon the Rock so you can be broken or the rock will fall on you. Matthew 23:12 in the Amplified version confirms this by saying: "Whoever exalts himself [with haughtiness and empty pride] shall be **humbled** (brought low), and whoever **humbles** himself [whoever has a modest opinion of himself and behaves accordingly] shall be raised to honor."

Our greatest example of One, who humbled Himself, being raised to honor is in fact . . . Jesus! His extreme humility and lowliness is the pattern and model we should imitate in our lives. Philippians 2:5-10 gives us one of many important reasons why Jesus is to be our example of humility. Let's take a brief look at this passage from the Amplified Bible. It reads:

*"Let this same attitude and purpose and [humble] mind be in you which was in Christ Jesus: [Let Him be your example in humility:] Who, although being essentially one with God and in the form of God [possessing the fullness of the attributes which make God], did not think this equality with God was a thing to be eagerly grasped or retained, **But stripped Himself [of all privileges and rightful dignity]**, so as **to assume the guise of a servant (slave)**, in that He became like men and was born a human being. And after He had appeared in human form, **He abased and humbled Himself [still further] and carried His obedience to the extreme of death, even the death of the cross!** Therefore [because He stooped so low] God has highly exalted Him and has freely bestowed on Him the name that is above every name, That in (at) the name of Jesus every knee should (must) bow, in heaven and on earth and under the earth."*

Perhaps one of the greatest things we can learn from this passage is that Jesus lived a lifestyle of humility and because of that, people of God, He was rewarded with an everlasting, eternal reward that cannot be compared to any earthly accolades one could ever receive.

Before I continue, let me share with you a couple of the things I have personally done and do as a way to humble myself. I'd first like to mention that there have been many times when I intentionally pushed my vision to the side in order to serve others. This was because I wanted to make sure I never went forth ministering in vanity or thinking because I was talented it had to be my time to be recognized, applauded or in the spotlight. I instead, made sure that all I had been gifted with was used for the benefit of others. To this day, there are those who can testify to this. I have also taken on many assignments where I already knew upfront that the only thing I'd receive would be the joy of simply being able to be a blessing to others.

I have even denied honorariums, gifts, dinners, etc. Why? It is one of the ways I choose to humble, strip, and deny myself. Although, I have felt the temporary pain of denying my flesh, it was still well worth it because in the spirit realm, where it really matters, I gained so much more.

Yes, you may have to experience great pain and make great sacrifices in order to intentionally humble yourself. Despite that, please know the pain will be incomparable to your ultimate eternal gain. You shall receive glory as a result of doing so.

As I close, I'd like to reflect on what Proverbs 11:2 tells us. The Amplified Bible reads: *"When swelling and pride come, then emptiness and shame come also, but with the humble (those who are lowly, who have been pruned or chiseled by trial, and renounce self) are skillful and Godly wisdom and soundness."*

Walk It Out and Focus Questions

> ➤ If you desire to humble yourself or to become more humble, the key factor is your ability to know yourself because then you can quickly identify and act on the things you know would be beneficial in enabling you to deny, strip, and humble yourself.
> ➤ Look up 1 John 2:15-16 in different versions of the bible, and then write down what you discover about this passage. For example, note if the passages impact you in any way or if you learned anything new about pride?

Let's Agree in Prayer: *Father, please help me to meditate often on Philippians 2:3-10 so this may help me to live out a lifestyle of humility and know that by doing so I will be sharing in a portion of my Lord's suffering but also sharing in a portion of His glory. In Jesus' name I pray. Amen.*

Chapter 8: May the Perfected Will of the Lord Be Done!

Trust in the Lord Because He Knows What Is Best

The words "May the perfected will of the Lord be done" is a short but very powerful, profound, and effective prayer. In its simplicity it means: **"Let only the perfected will of the Lord come to pass in every matter."** This is a prayer I pray so much that it has become a part of many of my daily conversations, and I use it as a way to guard against "you name it". One thing about being an artist in the public's eye is that sometimes you will get sincere comments, suggestions, ministry invites, etc. but at other times, you may also get a bunch of what I'd like to call just "plain fluff". This fluff, unfortunately, can even come from those within the Christian community. Fact is, sometimes people are moved only by their emotions so if you're not careful and discerning, you could be moved by their emotions as well.

Therefore, as a way to help protect and guard my heart from the "hype" of others, as well as my own foul motives at times, when anything is presented to me I simply say and pray out loud, "Oh, okay. May the perfected will of the Lord be done." When I pray and say this, what I'm doing is instantly taking whatever is being presented to me and giving it quick, fast, and in a hurry over to the Lord. He is the only all-knowing One. Furthermore, by doing this, I'm also giving Him full permission to filter through everything so that the only decisions I make and the outcomes line up with His perfected will concerning that matter.

On the other hand, let me also state that although some offers, suggestions, comments, etc. you receive may be pure and filled with greatness, it still may not be the perfected, divine will of God for you to do and/or the right timing for you to do it. So if that's the case but you do it anyway, you may end up doing good deeds instead of fulfilling a part of your destiny. Honestly, I don't know about you, but as for me, I don't have that kind of time to waste which is why this prayer definitely comes in handy for me.

In 1 Corinthians 10:23 in the Amplified Bible the Apostle Paul said something very profound: *"All things are legitimate [permissible--and we are free to do anything we please], but not all things are helpful (expedient, profitable, and wholesome). All things are legitimate, but not all things are constructive [to character] and edifying [to spiritual life]."*

Although I have had good people with good intentions approach me and tell me how they wanted to hook up with me to do this and that, since it was not the perfected will or timing of God, these experiences never came to pass. Guess what? You will experience the same thing at some time in your walk. Yet I was still protected in my heart because I pray and declare on a consistent basis, "May the perfected will of the Lord be done." So this is a prayer that keeps me guarded from the often emotional decisions made by others, but it also helps to keep my own spirit right so I don't become bound by anger, bitterness, frustration, etc. against those who may not come through with whatever it was they said they were going to do.

In praying this prayer, you will begin to notice how it will immediately make you take your focus off of people and place it on the One it should always be on anyway, God. You will also begin to see how it will send you straight to God to ask Him why certain things never took place. Another important thing to note about this prayer is that the more it's prayed the more you will eventually start to believe it and come to understand that the true reason why many things may have never happened was because God actually ANSWERED your prayer! This will certainly allow you to begin to witness in its fullness the degree that God is in control of your life since you turned it over to His control.

Now I'd like to share a testimony with you from someone who has put this prayer into action and who is the very one who inspired me to share this prayer with you.

Testimony:

"May the perfected will of the Lord be done." These nine words have changed my life forever. I can't begin to tell you what peace this prayer has given me. All of my life I have relied on man and what man would do or would not do for me. I've also relied on my own expectations as to what I thought should or should not happen in my life. So as a result, I like many, let myself down because I allowed it. Never once, did I think about the great peace God could give me, if only I relied on Him sooner and on, "May the perfected will of the Lord be done". My introduction to this great gift of peace came from my beautiful, God-fearing daughter, Sepia. She had listened to me tell her on many occasions how, this and that person was so eager to help me in many of the projects I've endeavored to complete for God's glory, only to hear me come right back and tell her how many of the things and people never worked out. I found myself having to work it out alone, or so I thought. Because of the disappointment I felt, I covered up my pain with the smiles of, "That's okay", "I'll get it done", but inside I was really greatly disappointed. Then Sepia revealed to me how if I would just allow God to handle all things in my life by praying and saying out loud "May the perfected will of the Lord be done," I'd no longer be lifted high one moment, only to be thrown down low the next all because of man, and/or situations. Sure enough, once I received my daughter's words of wisdom wholeheartedly, my life has never been the same. I now feel great peace as I said earlier and experience great joy in all that I do. When things are tough, I stand in knowing my Lord and Savior "has me". I now say everyday in every area of my life, "May the perfected will of the Lord be done," and then turn whatever may be going on in my life over to Him while I go on holding on to the peace that only God can give. So I'd like to encourage you to go and live for God's glory while praying and standing on "May the perfected will of the Lord be done!"

India Hines
Founder of No Junk Productions
Better known as Mommy to my Daughter Sepia

Walk It Out and Focus Questions

> ➢ Have you ever been told by others this and that would happen, but then it didn't? If so, how did you feel about the situation and toward those who even made the suggestion(s)?
> ➢ Look up Proverbs 4:23. What does it tell us to do? Do you see how this prayer could help us with accomplishing what Proverbs 4:23 encourages us to do? If so, how?
> ➢ Because of the effectiveness of this prayer, "May the perfected will of the Lord be done," I'd highly recommend you to store this prayer away in your "treasure chest" and

when you pray it, make sure you pay close attention to the power and results of this prayer.

Let's Agree in Prayer: *Lord, I pray no matter how badly I may want something to come to pass or how good some things may appear, if it is not Your perfected will for my life then I give You total permission to shut it down so by no means will it come to pass. For I have chosen by decreeing and declaring this prayer that I will trust in Your perfected will alone to be done in my life. In Jesus' name I pray. Amen.*

Chapter 9: You Need Power not Just Talent

Only the Anointing of God Destroys Yokes

Although there are many people who can undeniably operate out of their talents and skills, very few operate out of the power of God. Why? Talents are given and skills are learned, but the anointing of God costs a dear price. Many would rather not have to pay the price to receive it. Now, what exactly is the cost? I'm glad you asked! It's the cost of being obedient to God. Acts 5:32 confirms this when it says His Holy Spirit (which is His power) is given to those who obey Him. There are a lot of people nowadays coming into the church who are very, very, talented, but God's anointing is what definitively separates those who've paid the price of obedience from those who have not.

Being talented can get you much applause and give you the ability to hype a crowd, but on the other hand, talent cannot give you discernment, which is defined as the ability to operate skillfully in Godly wisdom. Neither will talent give you the power of God needed to bring about deliverance in the lives of others. However, having God's anointing, His Spirit of truth and power can.

When you have God's anointing resting upon your life, in case you don't know, God allows His signs, wonders and miracles, to be demonstrated through those He's anointed.

Acts 5:12 confirms this by saying: *"And through the hands of the apostles **many signs** and **wonders** were done among the people..."*

> **Though being talented can get you much applause, talent, however, cannot give you God's wisdom or the power you need in order to deliver others.**

And why is this? As I stated earlier in the sub-title of this chapter, it's only the anointing of God that destroys yokes. In plain terms, a "yoke" is a condition (spiritual and [sometimes] physical), state of mind, or anything that binds or hinders non-believers and believers from doing the will of God. It is a hardship or undue burden or weight, which God never intended for us to carry.

Let's take a look at the life of David because he's a perfect example of one who operated not only in his talent but also in the power of God. Let's read about this in, 1 Samuel 16:14-23. It reads:

*"But the Spirit of the Lord departed from Saul, and a distressing spirit from the Lord troubled him. And Saul's servants said to him, "Surely, a distressing spirit from God is troubling you. Let our master now command your servants, who are before you, to seek out a man who is **a skillful player on the harp. And it shall be that he will play it with his hand when the distressing spirit from God is upon you, and you shall be well**." So Saul said to his servants, "Provide me now a man who can play well, and bring him to me." Then one of the servants answered and said, "Look, I have seen a son of Jesse the Bethlehemite, who is skillful in playing, a mighty man of valor, a man of war, prudent in*

*speech, and a handsome person; **and the LORD is with him**." Therefore Saul sent messengers to Jesse, and said, "Send me your son David, who is with the sheep." And Jesse took a donkey loaded with bread, a skin of wine, and a young goat, and sent them by his son David to Saul. So David came to Saul and stood before him. And he loved him greatly, and he became his armor bearer. Then Saul sent to Jesse, saying, "Please let David stand before me, for he has found favor in my sight." **And so it was, whenever the spirit from God was upon Saul, David would take a harp and play it with his hand. Then Saul would become refreshed and well, and the distressing spirit would depart from him**."*

This portion of scripture is extremely relevant to the point I am trying to make. That point is that we need God's power not just talent. It certainly justifies the reason why it deserves an in-depth look. I'd really like you to know this nugget. God actually desires all of us to walk in His power so He may ultimately receive glory from our witness and the demonstration of His true wonder working power. I must tell you, there are a few things that could prevent us from receiving this power. The first is disobedience. If we appoint ourselves to do certain things for God instead of allowing Him to appoint us and if we're not witnesses of Jesus, things like this could definitely block God's power from being transferred to us. Think about it. Why should God arbitrarily entrust the awesomeness of His power to anyone who is basically still out there doing his or her own thing?

I remember an interesting time in my life where I basically went blank and couldn't quite understand what made me any different than the next Christian, but God brought about quick clarity to my state of confusion by allowing me to hear one of His servants. This person explained to me that it's the personal level of commitment I've made with the Lord that separates me from the next. My goodness! When I heard that, I was instantly freed from my moment of amnesia. Immediately many of my past and present vows, times of consecration, commitments, etc. all started to flood my mind helping to validate the truth in that statement and proved to me that even though it appears that all Christians are on the same playing field, in reality the level of commitment made to God creates a clear-cut difference.

It was also brought to my attention how there are Christians who've never made a vow unto the Lord, and who may never make one because they are entirely too comfortable in their fleshly desires. Many won't give up anything, not even for God. This is exactly what I am referring to when I say there are those who would rather not have to pay the costs of obedience even if it means receiving and walking in a greater level of the power of God.

Make no mistake about it, it is a very high price to pay when we must die to the desires of our flesh in order to please God; however, I can truly testify that the rewards are much, much greater than the sacrifices because God is forever faithful to His word.

Hebrews 11:6 tells us: "*But without faith it is impossible to please Him, for he who comes to God must believe that He is, **and that He is a rewarder of those who diligently seek Him**.*"

I have personally witnessed His faithfulness, and this is why I wrote this chapter to encourage us to do the things that He asks of us. We should never get caught up in our skills, abilities, or anything else for that matter; instead, always stay in constant pursuit of God's power to fortify our skills.

We must remember that 1 Corinthians 4:20 tells us, "*For the kingdom of God **is not in word but power**.*"

Walk It Out and Focus Questions

> Allow your obedience to God to be your primary focus since God will not only give you the skill but also give you His power with that skill to destroy yokes off of the lives of others.
> Never think because someone is talented that they have God's power operating in them. Just as God gives His power to those who are His, the devil also gives his power to those who've sold their souls to him.
> Please read Luke 24:36-49. This portion of scripture talks about when Jesus revealed Himself to His disciples. What did Jesus tell them to do before they went out and witnessed in His name? The answer is found in verse 49.
> Can you think of any other biblical examples besides David who were also used by God to do signs, wonders and miracles? If so, who are they and what did they do?

Let's Agree in Prayer: *Father, since truly Your power is the only thing that can destroy yokes and set the captives free, please reveal to me whatever it is I need to do in order to operate in this yoke-destroying, burden-removing power in a greater way. In Jesus' name I pray. Amen.*

Chapter 10: Stop Looking For the Applause

Desire God's Approval More Than Man's

If we're the type of people who are always looking to receive applause and accolades for whatever we do for God then that's a clear indication we are still trying to please flesh, either ours and/or others. It also means we're not yet a "set apart" vessel for God to use for His glory. I say this because looking to receive applause is something of this world; something expected in order to stroke your own ego. However, I once heard someone say, "If all we do is look to receive praise from man then eventually all we'll be able to become is what man would have for us to be instead of what God has predestined us to be."

Another reason why we as set apart artists can't allow ourselves to be stuck on trying to receive praise from man (be applauded) is because, quite frankly, we may not always get it, especially if what we're doing is ministering through our gifts and talents with God's anointing and not entertaining. For instance, if we're speaking the word of God and or displaying it, sharing our testimonies and the love of Christ with others who don't know or have an intimate relationship with Him, then surely the people will look at what we do in a different way because we are not catering to their flesh or always making them feel good. Hence, the reason why I said we may not always get applauded. We could in fact, get a smile, frown, see tears, and hear laughter. We just never know.

> **You may not always receive applause If what you are doing is ministering through your gifts and talents opposed to entertaining.**

Something else to be mindful of, though it's rarely the case, is this, there may even be times where we get "booed". This is because everybody may not be so willing to accept our message particularly if it's the gospel or exposes the sin in their lives or the lives of others. However, if we were to get booed, we need to be reminded of how Jesus, Himself, was also rejected (See Luke 9:22.), and know if we are rejected they're not rejecting us but instead rejecting the Christ in us. It also doesn't mean we failed or what we set out to deliver was not received because of man's outward response to us; **it is only God who knows the hearts of man**. This includes the hearts of those who clap as well because in case you didn't know, hand claps can even be deceptive because they may only be given as a way to hurry us off the platform. It happens. This is one of the main reasons why we've all been advised to do whatever it is we do **for the glory of God alone** and not for man.

Let me tell you about a situation where I honestly felt completely rejected after I ministered. It was after I shared my testimony at a certain conference. I was instructed by God not only to tell about my past experiences and drama but to also to make sure I spoke about Him since He, alone, was my true Deliverer. So out of obedience, that's exactly what I did. But in doing so, I noticed that the leaders of this particular organization did not respond to me whatsoever during my presentation or when I was done, and I must say that was quite a challenge for me because I had just bore my soul publicly.

I did receive a thunderous applause from the youth and most importantly, I knew beyond a shadow of a doubt, many had been delivered right there on the spot because of the power of God and my testimony. Yet, it still felt like I had just been stoned. I give God praise because He didn't have to, but He ministered to me by letting me know how very pleased He was with what I had done. He also let me know the reason why I felt rejected was because I went against their system. They thought I was going to show up with book knowledge, but when I showed up with God and my real life testimony, it surprised them. Nevertheless, to God it was not a surprise; hence, the reason why God made a way out of no way for me to be present. The result of my obedience with this particular situation ended up being that later God allowed me to receive a thank you letter from this organization, an honorarium, and many different testimonies as a result of having been present. However, I repeat, it still was not a comfortable situation for me when I was going forth.

When I look back on what I thought was nothing but a horrible situation because I had not received the kind of response/praise I thought I should've received, I undeniably learned so much from it.

First of all, I was reminded not to look to man to receive praise but instead to look to God for His approval. I also learned how to encourage myself in the Lord whenever I'm in situations like that. There definitely may be times when God does not allow us to see in any way, shape, or form the results of our labor, but in the end He will show us and will make it well worth it.

Now, if by chance you were an entertainer in the world before coming to Christ or even if not, clearly accepting that you cannot expect to receive applause could be a challenge especially since we are naturally people who like to be praised and recognized for the things we do. Yet, for those of us who are in Christ, we have to make sure we stay focused solely upon looking to God to receive His praise rather than man's. By doing so, we learn to stay in God's divine order, but it will also help us to maintain a protected heart knowing that we are accomplishing the will of God for our lives and not just doing what we do to receive man's consent, approval and support.

Before I close, let me reiterate this: stop looking for applause! I am not saying we should not appreciate the sincere applause we will receive many times because we most definitely should. However, what I am saying is that we should be careful we don't get stuck and engulfed in the praise of others because they are not our ultimate judge when it's all said and done.

Walk It Out and Focus Questions

> ➢ When you're in need of encouragement or praise if you refuse to look to man but instead to God to hear Him tell you, "Well done, thy good and faithful servant," you will not go wrong.
> ➢ In John 7:7, we see how Jesus did not look to the world to receive praise but instead said the world would hate Him. Why did Jesus say this?
> ➢ When we are mindful of how there have been people in other countries and even right now who are being stoned, beaten, jailed, tortured, murdered, etc. because they desire to glorify God with their gifts, something we do freely in America, this should definitely keep you from getting caught up in applause and accolades but to simply be grateful you're able to minister in the present without that type of persecution.

Let's Agree in Prayer: *Lord, since Your praise is the only true praise that really matters, please place an earnest desire within me to hunger and thirst for my approval to come first and foremost from You. In Jesus' name I pray. Amen.*

Chapter 11: Why I Am Not a Performer

The Significance of a Name

The reason why I am not a performer, simply put, is because I did not come to entertain anybody! I've come way too far in Christ to have folks sit back and look at what I've sacrificed to do for God like I'm some kind of show. No! I take what I do for Christ very seriously, and my entertaining days are long over and were over once I yielded to the call of Christ on my life. When I was in the world, yes, I did use my talents to perform, and I used them to receive glory. However, now when I go forth in ministry, I use my gifts and talents in a manner that gives all the glory to God and to God alone.

1 Corinthians 1:29-31 tells us: *"That no flesh should glory in His presence. But of Him you are in Christ Jesus, who became for us wisdom from God—and righteousness and sanctification and redemption— that, as it is written, "**He who glories, let him glory in the Lord**."*

One of the reasons I believe so many in the Body of Christ still call us performers and entertainers is because many have not yet been able to see the true difference between what we do for Christ and what others do for the world. This, unfortunately, has largely been contributed to the fact that there are quite a few artists in the Body of Christ who operate under a show spirit. Yes, they operate with a performer and entertainer mindset, which is rooted in the spirit of pride. The result is that some have intentionally done whatever it took to make sure they received the attention they craved.

> **"When I yielded to the call of Christ upon my life, my entertaining days we're then finished as well."**

However, I believe once we, as artists, come into full agreement with God that we are no longer performers and entertainers but instruments to be used for His glory, we can then help educate the Body of Christ by displaying and living a lifestyle that represents the huge differences between those of us who serve Christ with our gifts and those who do not.

The Significance of a Name

Having done radio now for quite some time, I've heard an array of different names artists give themselves, and honestly, some have ministered to me while others have been plain confusing. I believe the ones that were confusing were due to the artists not knowing what all a name truly represents. Because of this, I chose to briefly discuss it in this chapter.

Titles, tags, and names are extremely important and especially when you're a child of God because whatever it is you are called or known by, the truth is, you will eventually start to take on the very nature of that name. This is why it is very crucial what we call ourselves and what we permit others to call us because God's word is true when it says: *"Death and life are in the power of the tongue, and those who love it will eat its fruit"* (Proverbs 18:21). Thus, if our name reflects life then life is what we will have; likewise, if our name reflects death then death is also what we will have.

If by chance you're not aware of this, God takes names awfully seriously and so should we! There are numerous occasions found throughout the bible where God changed the names of those who were called by Him and walked with Him. Why? He only wanted those people to operate in what He declared them to be. For example, God changed Abram to Abraham (which means father of many nations), Sari to Sarah (which means princess), Jacob to Israel, Saul to Paul, Simon to Peter, and the list goes on and on.

A name change with God was and is something very symbolic and meaningful. Interestingly enough, I've noticed how there are still many of us who've never gone through a name change. For instance, some artists have decided to keep their stage names, the names they used while using their talents in a worldly way. And though some have added a spiritual twist to it, I believe those names represent a counterfeit and probably are not what God would have them to use. To back up my theory, I refer to 2 Corinthians 5:17 the Amplified version which tells us: *"Therefore if any person is [ingrafted] in Christ (the Messiah)* **he is a new creation (a new creature altogether)**; *the old [previous moral and spiritual condition] has passed away.* **Behold the fresh and new has come!"**

So the new names I'm referring to here are ones where they not only reflect a change has occurred in us ---to us---, but they reflect the same thing to others as well.

Some of you may question my belief and say, "But I let go of my past, and that's what matters!" I believe if you haven't gone through a name change then *your past may not have let go of you.* See, when you operate with a new name, it's a part of your fresh new start. Again, I'm talking about stage names here. For example, when I used my talents for the world (in the secular arena), I used my middle name, Eyesha, primarily because it was very popular at the time. Since I liked the attention it brought, I used it at every performance and was proud of it too. Later on, I also used the name Anonymous because at that time I didn't want anybody to know anything about me. I hope you can see how each name I used had its own separate baggage, mess, and memories attached.

Once I was fully converted and became a believer, God started to minister to my heart how He wanted me to begin to use my first name, Sepia. My first name was a name I never used a lot because I had low self-esteem and didn't have the confidence needed to help people pronounce it correctly. However, once God started to flood me with His love, I later received the confidence I needed and eventually began to feel honored every time I was even given the opportunity to share it with others. In fact, my name change still continues to impact my life to this very day because every time I'm able to say it, I'm reminded over and over again that for a long time, because of my bondage, I once could not. But now I praise God that I can because it represents my freedom from certain things.

I know firsthand the freedom one can experience due to receiving a new name from God; this is why I encourage others to receive one as well. I believe wholeheartedly, there is a "set apart" name, set aside for all who desire to reflect how they have experienced the TOTAL change in Christ that 2 Corinthians 5:17 talks about.

Walk It Out and Focus Questions

> ➤ Jeremiah 9:24 says we have permission to glory in who? Why?
> ➤ As a way to deliberately get you to think about what your name means, what do you call yourself and why?
> ➤ If you haven't already gone through a name change and feel led to do so, ask God what you should be called or known as especially since now you know that names are very serious to God.
> ➤ Even when we say things like, "I'm going to perform at such and such place." or "I'm going to do a show.", or "I'm scheduled to entertain." , etc. these are words we have to be very cautious about because by using them, we are to some extent sowing seeds into the entertainment mentality I spoke about earlier. Instead, we should say, *I'm going to minister or simply BE.*
> ➤ Whenever I work with Christ-Centered artists instead of calling them performers and entertainers, I call them creative artists and encourage others do the same. Creative means characterized by originality, and imaginative. Our heavenly Father is our Creator, and we are His created who are creative just like He is. I find the name creative artists to be quite fitting.

Let's Agree in Prayer: *Father, if there is anything within me that desires to receive glory opposed to giving You all the glory, please reveal it to me so I may repent, turn from my ways to do it Your way. Also, please help me to continually welcome my complete newness in You. In Jesus' name I pray. Amen.*

Chapter 12: Surprise, You Are a Minister!

You've Already Been Ordained by God

L isten, before you close this book thinking I've lost my mind all because I said you're a minister, please give me a chance to explain. I guarantee that your life will be changed in a very radical way if you haven't already laid hold of this truth, but before I continue, let me say it once more, "You are a minister." That means you have entered into a divinely ordained training that will last forever. Yes, you, wearing the baggy jeans, hat to the back, tie or bowtie, suit wearing man or woman, DNKY, Coach carrying sista, etc., are a minister. Actually if you do anything for God, the truth is, you're a minister, a minister of the gospel of Jesus Christ.

I know a lot of us have shied away from being called a minister primarily because of all we've thought it entails. In actuality, what a minister means is to be "**a servant**". So, if you are serving Christ in any way, a minister is who you are, whether you do so through rap, dance, song, art, ushering, teaching, sowing, writing, business, etc. You're a minister.

The reason I'm sharing this with you is because, most assuredly, it is high time that we all come to understand in a greater capacity the seriousness of our call. Yet before we can do that, I realize we must know who we are, and then what the call even is. So let's begin with being who we are.

> **It is high time that we all come to understand the seriousness of our call.**

The word of God tells us in 1 Peter 2:9 that we are a: *"...chosen generation, **a royal priesthood**, a holy nation, His own special people, that we may proclaim the praises of Him who called us out of darkness into His marvelous light."*

Can you see how it is God who has declared us to be a **royal priesthood**? This scripture also lets us know what we're supposed to be doing and that is proclaiming the praises of Him who has called us out of darkness into His marvelous light.

Before I go any further, let me first state this to all who don't know this. God does not dwell in temples made with hands; (See Acts 17:24) however, He dwells within us.

1 Corinthians 3:16 tells us: *"Do you not know that you are the temple of **God** and that the Spirit of **God** dwells in you?"*

Therefore, since God's Spirit dwells within us, here are a few more surprises you ought to know. First of all, your pulpit is mobile; it's with you wherever you go. Secondly, the message you've been called to present is the good news of the gospel in whatever creative form God has given you. Thirdly, your robe is supposed to be the robe of righteousness (See Isaiah 61:10.). Also, your congregation is whatever audience you go before whether it's one or a million. Certainly, one of the most important things you need to know is that the overall ministry God has given you is the ministry of **reconciliation**.

Let's take a look at what 2 Corinthians 5:18 in the Amplified version says: *"But all things are from God, Who through Jesus Christ reconciled us to Himself [received us into favor, brought us into harmony with Himself]* **and gave to us the ministry of reconciliation** *[that by word and deed we might aim to bring others into harmony with Him]."*

Therefore, from the few scriptures I listed above, it is clear that we've already been *called*, *commissioned* and *ordained* by God. Thus, because of this call, it is an absolute must that we release the mentality of thinking we're just singers, dancers, writers, poets, mimes, and entrepreneurs because that is not the total truth. Our talents are a part of us not the whole of us; we are much, much more as ministers of the gospel of Jesus Christ.

In fact, God has entrusted His people, His flock into our care for the sole purpose of feeding His sheep, and this is something we will all be held accountable for since we've already been commissioned by God in Mark 16:15. The Amplified version reads: *"Go into all the world and preach and publish openly the good news (the gospel) to every creature [of the whole human race]."*

In writing this chapter, I really wanted to caution you against not walking out the fullness of your call maybe because you're waiting on man to take notice of what God has already done in and through your life. Because hear me, if you don't walk out your call, this will ultimately cause you to be disobedient to God. As a side note, we do not need man to lay hands on us, give us a piece of paper stating we're minister such and such in order to be and do whatever it is God is calling us to do. Don't get me wrong; it is an awesome experience to be ordained by one of God's generals. However, it is not a necessity in order for us to be obedient to the call of God on our lives.

For that reason to those of us who've said "I'll step up in this and that area of my character and/or responsibility once I get ordained," here's the truth. You've already been ordained by the God of all heaven and earth. So now is the time for not only you but for all us to arise to the higher standard to which Christ is calling us since we hold the same mantle if not greater for the call, charge, and commission given to us as our very own pastors. This call has essentially been given to the whole Body of Christ. Unfortunately, only a few in comparison to the whole has chosen to accept it. Yet, the commission (Matthew 28:19-20) still stands and applies to us all.

I remember the first time I experienced being called into who I am. It all started when I attended my first evangelism team meeting, and the Elder greeted my whole group by saying "Welcome ministers of the gospel of Jesus Christ." When I heard those words, it felt like my heart dropped dead into my stomach, and I thought to myself, "Minister? Yea right! You've got to be kidding; surely you're not talking about me. I'm just a rapper." To my surprise, he *was* talking to me, and the more I heard him call me a minister, the more I eventually started to accept it. Not long after that, I was able to witness myself become it.

I noticed after I finally accepted the call to be a minister that everything about me started to change for the better because I finally knew who I really was. Because of the drastic change I witnessed in my own life by accepting this call, not to mention receiving the very truth of God, I felt compelled to pronounce, declare, and settle in the heavens above and in every place beneath how you also are without a doubt, a minister of the gospel of Jesus Christ. Please receive, NOW, if you haven't already, your impartation to **GO** and **BE**.

Walk It Out and Focus Questions

➤ As a way to help you embrace your call as a minister, please memorize and study the scriptures I listed in this chapter: 1 Peter 2:9, 1 Corinthians 3:16, Mark 16:15, and Matthew 28:19-20.

➤ Confess daily that you are a minister of the gospel of Jesus Christ and that you minister through (whatever it is you do). You'll be surprised at what the power of those few words will do.

➤ Use a concordance to look up the word minister to see how and when it was used throughout the bible. Also, jot down some of the different ways Jesus ministered to the people.

➤ What would you do differently or even begin to do if you had known before today you were already a minister? Whatever your answer to this question is, I'd strongly encourage you to begin to do whatever it is you said.

➤ Refuse to allow fear to prevent you from receiving your God-given call in Christ. 1 John 4:18 says: …"fear involves **torment**," and this torment is not God's will for our lives. In fact, it's the exact opposite. So whenever fear tries to rise up, cast it down by quoting the truth found in 2 Timothy 1:7 which says: "For God has not given us a spirit of fear, but of power and of love and of a sound mind."

Let's Agree in Prayer: *Heavenly Father, for such a time as this, I know I am here to fulfill Your call on my life, so please help me to be loosed from any bondage that would dare try to hinder me from doing so. Please help me to continually recognize that the call on my life is a priestly one, which requires priestly responsibilities. Help me to be found faithful in both the call and the responsibilities. In Jesus' name I pray. Amen.*

Chapter 13: Don't be Fooled There Is a Church Industry

Guard Yourself Against the Counterfeit

When I say there's a "church industry," I mean just that! There's a full-fledged church industry where there are those who conduct their ministries/churches just like the ways of the world. I wrote this chapter as a heads up so all the up and coming ministers and those currently in ministry would know and not be fooled. So, I'll say it again for emphasis: There is a church industry!

This industry is set up to get, get, get, at whatever cost necessary, even if it is at the cost of souls. They'll lie, steal, talk you under the ground behind your back, and then as I have once heard someone say pump you up just like a basketball in your face to flatter even the truth out of you, if you let them.

I like the way Psalm 12:2 says what I am expressing. The Amplified version reads: *"To his neighbor each one speaks words without use or worth or truth; with flattering lips and double heart [deceitfully] they speak."*

Seriously, there are a lot of folks who do things in the name of God, yet God is not their Source. They depend on themselves, their businesses or ministries as their Source. Part of this is essentially due to the fact that some feel as though their ministry, church or company is all they have. This is the reason they run it with the attitude that they, themselves, must make things happen opposed to allowing Jesus to be their all in all and make things happen for them.

> **There are a lot of folks who do things in the name of God yet, God is not their source for they themselves, business, or ministry are.**

Another thing for you to be aware of is this; when you have the Spirit of God resting upon your life, people will undoubtedly try to get you to be a part of their "stuff" all because they know if you do, their ministry, business, or vision will grow. Beware! With some people, it's for **their glory** and not for God's. This is how I quickly realized I needed to keep myself protected from the world's industry, but I also needed to keep myself protected from the church industry as well. I mean seriously, I had to declare to both God and the world, "I've come way too far to protect His glory on my life to be yoked with only a counterfeit or "perpetrator" of Him and miss out on my own soul salvation." No, I told the Lord I'm not having it because as for me, I'll stay unknown, in the background before I let anybody misuse, abuse, or pimp what God has given to me.

In fact, even the Lord, Himself, has tried to warn us about the fakes and phonies by saying: *"Not everyone who says to Me, Lord, Lord, will enter the kingdom of heaven, but he who does the will of My Father Who is in heaven. Many will say to me on that day, Lord, Lord, have we not prophesied in your name and driven out demons in your name and done many mighty works in your name? And then I will say to them openly (publicly), I never knew you; depart from me, you who act wickedly [disregarding My commands]"* (Matthew 7:21-23 AMP).

The truth is, the church industry is what I'd like to call a disguise because it's where satan, himself, actually stands as an angel of light (2 Corinthians 11:14) anxiously awaiting to accept us right on in to his program. Yes, his mission is to promote us, put us on platforms all across this world, and of course, even pay us more money than we've ever even imagined. However, if we allow ourselves to be lured into his deception, when it's all said and done, we will not be able to claim ignorance or use the excuse, "But God, they said it was for your name." No! God is going to hold us all accountable, and this will include who or whatever we allow ourselves to be yoked with as well as what we did or did not have the ability to discern.

A great example of this can be found in 1 Kings 13:1-29. (Please read that passage of scripture.) This chapter tells us about a situation where there was a young prophet of God who literally lost his life by being deceived by an older prophet. Although when you read this you may ask, "Well, why didn't this young prophet just listen to what had God told him to do?" Here's the reason: the young prophet thought like any of us could have thought that since the older man was a prophet, he could just believe and trust him. However, what this young prophet didn't know was that the older prophet was lying to him in order to get him off the "obedience track" he was on with God. The sad news is . . . it worked.

This is why, personally, I believe it's critical we all stay in a regular state of consecration. Something I'll discuss more in detail in the chapter entitled, "God Is Calling Us to Be Holy-Set Apart." But the reason I say this is because when we live a lifestyle of consecration, we are then guaranteed to operate in a greater level of discernment which in return will enable us to distinguish between good and evil and know what's really for Jesus, opposed to things that just have His name thrown all over it.

Matthew 7:15-20 tells us to: "*Beware of false prophets, who come to you in sheep's clothing, but inwardly they are ravenous wolves. You will know them by their fruits. Do men gather grapes from thorn bushes or figs from thistles? Even so, every good tree bears good fruit, but a bad tree bears bad fruit. A good tree cannot bear bad fruit, nor can a bad tree bear good fruit. Every tree that does not bear good fruit is cut down and thrown into the fire. **Therefore by their fruits you will know them**.*"

Since this church industry thing is undeniably a very real and serious issue, we need to keep our eyes and spirits extremely open at all times so we can discern and make a conscious decision right now to refuse to allow our gifts and talents to be bought or "pimped". Likewise, it's also very important that we only allow God, to make our names great so we are never deceived into thinking we're going forth in the name of Jesus yet all along we're working for satan.

Walk It Out and Focus Questions

> ➢ Be very cautious with whom and to what you allow yourself to be yoked. Just because someone uses the name of God or Jesus, only accept his or her belief system when you have first seen the character and fruit of God displayed.
> ➢ Allow Galatians 5:22-23 to be your guide in discovering what kind of fruit folks, companies, ministries, etc. are really bearing. The Amplified version reads: "*But the fruit of the [Holy] Spirit [the work which His presence within accomplishes] is love, joy (gladness), peace, patience (an even temper, forbearance), kindness, goodness (benevolence), faithfulness, Gentleness (meekness, humility), self-control (self-restraint, continence). Against such things there is no law [that can bring a charge].*"

➤ When tempted by the church industry to go astray, use this scripture as a weapon to defeat the attack: "*A GOOD name is rather to be chosen than great riches, and loving favor rather than silver and gold*" (Proverbs 22:1).

➤ Rid yourself of the outright deception of thinking that every door opened is from God because, truthfully, it may not be. It could be a door opened by satan, himself, in order to attempt to strategically get you off course. 1 Peter 5:8 AMP tells us: "*Be well-balanced (temperate, sober of mind), **be vigilant and cautious at all times; for that enemy of yours, the devil, roams around like a lion roaring [in fierce hunger], seeking someone to seize upon and devour.***"

Let's Agree in Prayer: *Father, please deliver me from **all** evil including that of the world and that of the church by keeping me far away from getting involved in anything that does not officially represent You and Your Kingdom. In Jesus' name I pray. Amen.*

Chapter 14: God Wants and Deserves All the Glory!

Let Nothing Steal God's Credit

For what the Lord God Almighty has already done and is going to do in our lives, He wants and deserves all the glory. I state this because not only is it true, but also because there will be times when God will allow us to support others in whatever they're doing for Him. However, if God, Who knows the hearts of man, sees someone or something is trying to steal His glory and/or sees we're looking to someone or something to give us glory/credit for what He, alone, has done, He will more than likely shut it down. Why? The answer is simple: God is a jealous God!

Exodus 20:5 tells us: *"You shall not bow down yourself to them or serve them; for I the Lord your God am a jealous God…"*

Likewise, if God notices that we are quenching or allowing others to quench the Him in us, or if we're involved in something that's causing us to compromise our walk with Him, or if the people we're serving (whether they're paying us or not) do not truly value our service, these are just a few things that could definitely prevent God from getting the maximum glory He is due. These things will possibly prompt Him to shut down certain things in our lives.

In fact, you might even be a part of something very successful, and yet the outcome may be something very much like what Abram (Abraham) experienced. He won the war (completed his assignment) but once he had done that, he did not accept a thing from man as a reward or that exalted himself, not even a shoelace. He did this **so that no one could be able to say, they made Him rich other than God** (Read Genesis 14).

> **If God, Who knows the hearts of man, sees someone or something is trying to steal His glory and/or sees we're looking to someone or something to give us glory/credit for what He, alone, has done, He will more than likely shut it down.**

Abraham had the proper attitude and posture toward winning a victory with the Lord God on his side. Here's one more thing to note specifically about Genesis 14:22-23. You can take absolutely nothing when you know without a doubt that God Almighty enabled you to get the victory or achieve a certain level of success. After all, He is the great **I AM**.

Since frustration could present itself in the lives of many as a result of God's desire **and right** to receive all the glory from us, I'd like to talk specifically about frustration for a minute. If for some reason you have become frustrated in whatever your God-given assignment is, one good question to ask yourself is, *"Have I been looking for my reward/inheritance/ "Canaan" to come from man and/or that assignment?"* If yes was your answer to this question, please be aware that your particular assignment may have never been meant by God to be used as a vehicle of provision. That's right! It may have simply been meant for you to serve while learning to trust God as your sole Provider.

Whether this is the case or not, it's still the reason why it would greatly benefit us to always remain extremely sensitive to the Lord concerning our assignments. That way we can know precisely when they're over. By staying sensitive to the Lord, most frustration can be prevented or alleviated by keeping us from operating outside of God's grace, will, and timing.

In Ecclesiastes 3:1 the Amplified version tells us: *"TO EVERYTHING there is a season, and a **time** for every matter or purpose under heaven."*

Look for the Signs

If you find yourself frustrated, complaining and/or starting to operate out of your flesh and not out of the Spirit of God, it could mean it's time for you to "separate to elevate" as Abram had to do. In Genesis 13:7, Abram was trying to take Lot along with him into his promise land but because that was not the perfected will of God, He stopped the provision in the land and allowed their herdsmen to be at war with one another. God permitted this to happen so that He could get Abram's attention and let him know it was time to separate so He could make his name great.

I referred to Genesis 13:7 because I wanted to bring to your attention how God can speak to us by or through His signs, but I must also point out that although He can speak to us all day and night by signs, if we're not in tune with His Holy Spirit, the fact is, we'll miss them (the signs) and Him.

Joshua 7 (Please read this chapter.) is another great chapter to reference regarding how God can speak to us by His signs because in that chapter you will see how the sin of one man caused the defeat of a whole army. This defeat, by the way, was without doubt a direct sign from God because Israel had always been accustomed to winning. Praise God! During Joshua's frustration and defeat, he chose to stop and pay closer attention to the sign because had he ignored it. We are told in verse 12, he would've lost the very presence of God if he hadn't destroyed the accursed thing. Remember the sin was not personally Joshua's, but he would've had to pay for it as if it were his own. It's a wonderful thing that he had the discernment to pay attention to that sign.

I'll speak about this again in the chapter entitled, "Let Us Not Grow Weary in Well Doing". I will go into detail about signs and frustration, which may also be known as weariness. Prayerfully, I shared enough on this subject to bring peace and clarity to those who were in need of it. Although I touched on a couple of different topics throughout this chapter, I hope you understand that the sole purpose for it was to convey to you that God wants and deserves all the glory. This discussion was also meant to demonstrate how He will do whatever He needs to do in our lives in order to make sure He gets just that. He's going to get the glory even if it means frustrating the "mess" out of us. Know that God merely wants our undivided attention so that we may receive His wisdom, make whatever adjustments are needed, and then return to giving Him the maximum glory He is due.

Walk It Out and Focus Questions

> ➢ Make sure whatever or whoever you serve, you never allow yourself to look to them or it as your all and all. Never forget how it was God, alone, who opened the doors for you to be positioned.
> ➢ Even when things are going well, it is wise to be aware that God wants to get and keep us in His predestined purpose for our lives. He can and may shift things on us in the blink of an eye. This is why it's best to always stay in the position of, *"Lord, I thank you for where I am currently; however, if it's Your will for me to make a shift, so be it.*

Your will be done." By maintaining this mindset, you're acknowledging that God is Lord over your life.

➢ In addition to paying close attention to God's signs, it's also very wise for us to stay in constant prayer for those we work with so the Lord can always keep us updated on their hearts and let us know whether we're winning the war or being defeated because of hidden sin or other things.

➢ In Isaiah 42:8, what are we told? Please look up this passage to locate the missing words. Isaiah 42:8 reads: "*I am the Lord; that is My name! And My _____ I will not give to another, nor My _____ to graven images.*"

Let's Agree in Prayer: *Father, help me never get caught up in anything or anyone more than You. Please help me to always stay attentive to Your leading that I may honor You as Lord over my life. And even when I'm forced out of my comfort zone, please help me to yield fully to Your will so I may give You the total glory You deserve from my life. In Jesus' name I pray. Amen.*

Chapter 15: There Is Only One Way!

Jesus Alone Paid the Price

I know this truth can come by way of only the Holy Spirit revealing it to us; however, I was still led to reinforce the fact that there is only one Way. One way to what? One way to God, and that way was made possible through Jesus Christ, His only begotten Son. Jesus is the Way! Yet, for some odd reason, we still only hear a lot of folks talk about God not His Son, who shed His blood on Calvary so that man's relationship with God could be restored.

In fact, to use God's name has become a very popular thing to do; some have used it out of the true pureness of God, but others are using it out of complete foulness for such things like boosting CD sales, the popular vote, ratings, etc. There are even a lot of famous people who use God's name but unfortunately, many have been deceived into thinking they can have a relationship with God without first acknowledging His Son's conception through the Holy Spirit, birth, death, burial, and resurrection. Some think they can love God but not obey His commandments.

Because of deception, I personally no longer get wooed or thrilled when I hear anybody, including the famous (Christian or not) use God's name in whatever they say or do. Basically, I've come to understand if I get stuck on the fact that folks are using God's name and don't check their fruit out, then I, like others, could easily be led astray.

In Matthew 7:16, we are told that *"we will know them by their fruit."*

There are even many religions who acknowledge there's a God, but it's when the name of Jesus is lifted that division arises. Why? Many believe Jesus was only another good man who did good deeds, and to some, He was just another prophet and the list continues on and on. Nonetheless, I believe, as Jesus questioned His disciples in Matthew 16:13-16 (Please read.), He is still questioning us today, asking, **"But who do you say that I am**?"

As a matter of fact, if you were to simply get into deeper conversations with some of the very same people who claim God this and God that, you may be completely shocked and surprised by what you'd hear them say about their belief in God and Jesus. I know I have heard some say all kinds of things like how they believe, "It doesn't matter who or what they go through to get to God just as long as they love Him." However, this belief, as many of us already know, isn't the truth by any means because Jesus was the only One who paid the price required to redeem us from our sins (Colossians 2:13-15). Another common misconception is how some say they believe God is too good of a God to send anyone to hell. For people who believe this, it is evident to me that they're not aware of God's history because the same God to whom they refer is the same One who once flooded this whole world, destroyed cities, and punished people for disobeying His commandments. There are many more mouth-dropping biblical examples of things He did and allowed because of His justice and wrath toward those who didn't believe.

When we really explore the truth, you can talk about God all day long, and no one will really care but just mention the name of Jesus, and you'll begin to see eyebrows raise, conflict will definitely enter the conversation and there will never be 100 percent agreement. Why? Point blank, Jesus brings about deliverance, and if Jesus is lifted and receives glory and acceptance on a massive scale, we'd all see a totally different world. You'd think this is a good thing, but God's Kingdom operates totally different from this world's system. People don't like change, even if it's for the better. No, they prefer to satisfy their flesh and please others even if it's destructive. This is why the world tries to silence the truth about Jesus the only Way.

God's will is still going to be done regardless!

If by chance there are any of you reading this chapter who still has doubts about Jesus being the one and only Way, I'd like us to close by reflecting on one weighty scripture that confirms this truth.

Colossians 1:19-20 reads: "*For it pleased the Father that in Him all the fullness should dwell, and by Him to reconcile all things to Himself, by Him, whether things on earth or things in heaven, **having made peace through the blood of His cross**.*" Amen. And it is so!

Walk It Out and Focus Questions

> ➢ In John 14:5-6, what was Jesus' response when Thomas said, "Lord, we do not know where you are going, and how can we know the way?"
> ➢ What does Acts 4:12 tell us about salvation?
> ➢ Please look up 1 John 5:11-12 to locate the missing words for this passage. 1 John 5:11-12 reads: "*And this is the testimony: God has given us eternal life, and this life is in his _____. He who has the ___ has life; he who does not have the ____ of God does not have life.*"

Let's Agree in Prayer: *Father, if I have any doubts about Jesus being the one and only Way to receive salvation in You, I pray for the faith and discernment to believe and receive the truth. If I've already been granted the blessedness to understand this mystery, I pray for You to use me wherever there's a need for clarity and wisdom about this great truth in the lives of others. In Jesus' name I pray. Amen.*

Chapter 16: Do You Have to Say the Name of Jesus?

The Answer Revealed

The answer to this question basically depends on who or what it is we are lifting because if we're lifting ourselves like some of us did when we were of this world, then the answer to this question is "*no*". However, if we're lifting the will of God, then the answer is "*yes*" because Jesus is who God is lifting.

Now before you think I'm too spiritual or overzealous because of what I just said, please stay with me. In doing so, you'll be able to truly understand what I mean in its totality and put this discussion in the proper perspective after reading this chapter in its entirety.

So, let's begin with the reason why God is lifting Jesus. God is lifting Jesus because as discussed in previous chapters, "There is only one Way." It is only through Jesus that we can receive eternal life. (Please read 1 John 5:11-12).

Philippians 2:9-11 in the Amplified version of the bible tells us: "**Therefore *[because He stooped so low] God has highly exalted Him* and has freely bestowed on Him the name that is above every name, That in (at) the name of Jesus every knee should (must) bow, in heaven and on earth and under the earth, And every tongue [frankly and openly] confess and acknowledge that Jesus Christ is Lord, to the glory of God the Father.**"

> "And whatever you do [no matter what it is] in word or deed, do everything in the name of the Lord Jesus and in [dependence upon] His Person, giving praise to God the Father through Him."
> **Colossians 3:17 AMP**

By looking at the truth from the above scripture, it is justifiable to say that those of us who claim to do "gospel" anything must refer to Jesus and outright proclaim His name or what we're doing is not gospel. The gospel is the "good news," and that good news is **JESUS**. Remember, Jesus is the way, the truth, and the life, and no one comes to the Father except through Him (John 14:6). Since this is the case, His name should be declared and *boldly* declared consistently by those who say we're gospel artists.

Be mindful that many times when we lift the name of Jesus, it will cause division. That's okay! Even Jesus, Himself, told us that it would be so.

Luke 12:51-53 from the Amplified Bible confirms this by saying: "*Do you suppose that I have come to give peace upon earth? No, I say to you, but rather **division**; For from now on in one house there will be five divided [among themselves], three against two and two against three. They will be divided, father against son and son against father, mother against daughter and daughter against mother, mother-in-law against her daughter-in-law and daughter-in-law against her mother-in-law.*"

We see from reading this passage that the division is intentional; it's meant to be that way because Jesus came to expose hearts, separate the wheat from the tares, light from the darkness, and knock those who are on the fence off to one side or the other, that, ultimately, some might be saved.

Although some artists have decided to intentionally leave Jesus out of whatever it is they are doing and try to please people, 1 John 2:23 warned us against doing this saying: "***Whoever denies the Son does not have the Father either; he who acknowledges the Son has the Father also.***" Moreover, since Jesus allowed Himself to be made a spectacle and to become the sacrificial lamb for our salvation, even dying on the cross, we all ought to at least do the same for Him by allowing ourselves to be stretched outside of our comfort zones in order to intentionally lift Him up. I mean after all, He deserves it.

Please don't misunderstand me and think I'm saying if you do not say the name "Jesus" in everything you do then it's not inspired by God or it's not the gospel because that's not what I'm saying. I'm fully aware that there are many of times when God through His creative nature can give you a whole song, skit, dance, poem, etc, about Him and/or His Son, and yet their names are not directly mentioned. However, even in that situation, I also know if your intention is to truly give God the glory by lifting Jesus then whatever you do it will still be quite obvious to all who it is you are lifting. Before I continue, let me say that I'm specifically speaking to the group of people who have other motives when they ask whether or not they really have to say the name of Jesus in whatever they do.

Honestly, I believe when you're in a relationship with someone who has really made an impact on your life, how could you not speak about him or her? Matthew 12:34 from the Amplified version says: …"*for out of the fullness (the overflow, the superabundance) of the heart the mouth speaks.*" Therefore, if Jesus has really impacted our lives the way we say He has, I would have to question how we could keep quiet about His splendor, glory and goodness?

There were times when Jesus was not spoken of in an outright way although He was present all along. There is proof of this in the Old Testament. There also were even numerous occasions in the New Testament where Jesus, Himself, stated how He was not to be spoken of because the time had not yet come for Him to be glorified (Matthew 16:20). However, because Jesus was obedient even to the death of the cross, God permitted Him to receive all the glory (Philippians 2:8-9). Therefore, we've been instructed by the word of God to do this: "***And whatever you do [no matter what it is] in word or deed, do everything in the name of the Lord Jesus and in [dependence upon] His Person, giving praise to God the Father <u>through Him</u>***" (Colossians 3:17 AMP).

Listen, whether we want to acknowledge this or not, we are in the last days and now is the day of salvation (2 Corinthians 6:2). Now is the time for those who are God's trumpets to blow as loudly as we can throughout this world in order that the gospel not only be heard but ultimately received. Although trumpets may not always sound pleasing to the ears of others when blown, they do accomplish the purpose for which they were created.

In conclusion, Jesus paid an incredible price for us to be liberated from the wages of sin, I look forward to the day where we, collectively, as creative artists will make the same bold statement as Paul did in Romans 1:16 when he said: "*I am not ashamed of the gospel of Christ, for it is the power of God to salvation for everyone who believes. . .*" Selah (meaning pause and calmly think on that).

Walk It Out and Focus Questions

> ➤ Take a look within. Can you honestly say that what you do for God creatively is done to lift God up but also to lift up Jesus, His Son? If not, why?
> ➤ What does 1 Corinthians 15:25 say about Jesus?

Let's Agree in Prayer: *Father, please strip away anything that would dare try to prevent me from lifting up Your Son, Jesus, to this world. And when I am tempted to keep silent, I pray that my remembrance of His blood shed on the cross will literally compel me to open my mouth in a much bolder way. In Jesus' name I pray. Amen.*

Chapter 17: We Do not Have to Compromise!

Keep Your Witness Pure

We do not have to compromise the gospel attempting to relate to others. That's right! We do not have to water down anything, be dim, gray, mixed with pepper or anything else for that matter to draw God's people. No! Jesus said, *"And I, if I am lifted up from the earth, will draw all peoples to Myself"* (John 12:32).

In all actuality, God desires for us to radiate with His glory, and there are many references in His word where He not only tells us to shine, but to shine brightly so that we stand out. This is why we have to beware because much of what has been said is *our* method to reach the lost has really become our compromise. We do not have to stoop below God's standards in order to draw others. All we need to do is stand tall so we can be a support system others can hold on to and climb up.

Matthew 5:16 the Amplified version tells us: *"Let your light **so shine** before men that they may see your moral excellence and your praiseworthy, noble, and good deeds and recognize and honor and praise and glorify your Father who is in heaven."*

Did you know that the challenge with this direct command coming to pass at a greater level is because of the worldly methods some have tried to use as a way to win the lost? It's true; many have compromised to the point of quenching the Spirit, dimming their light and hindering the gospel by trying to dress it up and make it appealing and palatable to everybody.

> **Beware because much of what has been said is our method to reach the lost has really become our compromise.**

However, I'd like to share this nugget with you: ***God is not into numbers like we may think He is.*** He's into hearts that can ultimately be purely devoted to His will. One prime example that comes to mind is when God flooded the whole world; He only allowed eight souls to be saved. When Jesus walked the earth, God only allowed a few to be directly touched by His ministry in comparison to the multitudes of people who came into contact with Him. Why was this? God already knew and knows, some will heed and some will not, but the question is, when will *we* accept that?

In fact, when Jesus walked upon this earth, His message was: *"Repent for the kingdom of God is at hand"* (Matthew 4:17). Jesus was bold in who He was, and His message was in no way, shape, or form dressed up, sweetened, or watered down. Yet, He still brought about MAJOR deliverance in the lives of many. This is why; personally, I believe we all are in need of a greater understanding about the power of God because this will help us stay focused and far away from the spirit of compromise, covered up in the excuse of, "I'm just trying to reach as many souls as I can!" In reality, if we were simply to BE who God called us to BE, it would allow God do what He does best, which is to draw others to Himself, through Jesus Christ.

Also, when I speak about compromise, I have heard many artists say over the years how they did not do gospel this or gospel that. Interestingly enough, some of the very same people I heard say that are now back in the world having sold their souls to satan. Why? Primarily because they didn't know who they were; they didn't have a true standard, or they wanted to represent Christ but also wanted to please the world and their flesh. Since they didn't quite want to blaze, they decided to stay neutral, become a flickering light or accept being a flame covered by a wet blanket only blowing smoke.

"Being positive" is what some call it.

Yet, I can't speak for anybody else, but as for me, everything I do is for the gospel's sake and: "*I am not ashamed of the gospel of Christ: for it is the power of God unto salvation to everyone that believeth*" (Romans 1:16). I'm also not ashamed to be called a gospel this, Christian that, or anything else associated with Christ for that matter. I say this because it is only because of Jesus that I am who I am. A lot of bad things have attached themselves to titles like these because of the compromise of others, but it's okay because if everybody were to shy away from being called titles emphasizing the name of Christ (the Anointed One) then nobody would witness how some are truly sold out to Him.

Leaders, in all seriousness, we're the ones who really have to choose what side we are on because there are no in-betweens. Either we will be light or darkness, cold or hot. God, Himself, desires that we were one or the other saying: "*I know your [record of] works and what you are doing; you are neither cold nor hot. Would that you were cold or hot! So, because you are lukewarm and neither cold nor hot, I will spew you out of My mouth!*" (Revelation 3:15-16 AMP).

The truth is when we straddle the fence; it only makes us look bad and confused. Though we may say things like, "Extreme sin, calls for extreme measures," Ecclesiastes 1:9 tells us: "*There is nothing new under the sun.*" Although the sin of others may be new to us, it is not new to God. Sin has been around long before we ever were and will continue to be around long after we're gone if Jesus doesn't return first. Thus, we have to stand knowing that as God has judged in the past, He will continue to judge continuously. After all, He is a God of justice.

In the meantime, our responsibility is to simply be like Noah, to stay focused on building the ark so when it is judgment time, we are not caught off guard and off post because we compromised. Let's take heed to what Matthew 5:13 tells us about being "the salt of the earth" so we do not lose our saltiness and are "*no longer good for anything, except to be thrown out and trampled by men.*"

Walk It Out and Focus Questions

> ➤ Because there's a lot of compromise nowadays, one way to protect yourself from much of the deception is to stay saturated in God's word so you can judge accordingly between what's right and wrong. Also, never discredit the Holy Spirit that lives within you when you feel something is not right. Refuse to do it, even if it may be widely accepted by others.
> ➤ What does 1Thessaloians 5:22 in the King James Version of the bible tell us to do?
> ➤ If whatever we're doing to reach the lost has the appearance of being evil, we may need to rethink our approach so God is glorified from our efforts instead of being mocked.

Let's Agree in Prayer: *Lord, please help me to be consistently led by Your Holy Spirit, alone, so when it comes to reaching out to others, I only touch whomever it is You'd have me to touch in the direct way You'd have for me to do so. I also pray now Lord for God-given ideas that will draw people to you instead of pushing them away because of my approach. Lord, help me not miss the one or the few by being too focused on trying to reach the many. In Jesus' name I pray. Amen.*

Chapter 18: We've Got This Thing Twisted

Make Sure It's God Who Ultimately Makes the Profit

Surprisingly, the church at large has been tricked into thinking that we can "straight preach" the uncompromising word of Christ, and sinners will come ever so readily to hear, support, or in some cases, buy it. Thinking they'll come and purchase what we claim to have done (in Jesus' name) to reach them by attending our gospel events, marriage, youth, and single conferences while paying astronomical amounts of money in order to receive truth is not acceptable for any believer or ministry. Trust me; the ones who do will be few and far between. Therefore, this is why I said, "We've got this thing twisted."

Let's look at what John 3:20 tells us because this scripture actually sums up and explains the very reason why many are not so quick to accept what we have to offer, the gospel. The Amplified version reads: "*Every wrong doer hates (loathes, detest) the light but shrinks from it, lest his works, his deeds, his activities, his conduct, be exposed and reproved.*" Based on this passage, if we really want to reach the lost, we should go where they are, or if we invite them out to something, we should at least make sure it's presented in a way that would leave little or no excuse for them not to come and receive Christ. I'm specifically referring to how we put a price on or sell and present the gospel when we freely received it, ourselves.

I bring this up because, honestly, there still are quite a few people out there in the "gospel industry" and church trying to make a profit for their own pockets instead of doing what they've been called to do in order to win and profit souls. Yet, Jesus told His disciples in Matthew 10:7-8 before sending them out, according to the Amplified version: "*And as you go, preach, saying, the kingdom of heaven is at hand! Cure the sick, raise the dead, cleanse the lepers, drive out demons. Freely (without pay) have received, freely (without charge) give.*"

For those of us who've received the life changing truth of Christ we ought to make sure we never use it as being our ticket out of anything other than hell itself.

Now before I continue, let me clearly state that I'm not saying we shouldn't receive honorariums, gifts, offerings, etc. Please hear me in the spirit; I'm talking about operating out of foul motives here. Although it may be a challenge to always know the right way of doing things because some of our leaders have gone astray when it comes to reaching out to sinners, in these last days I know that will and must definitely change. Mark my words; there is a mass remnant soon to arise, which will touch more souls than has ever been recorded out of their true desire to share the "good news" by whatever means necessary (in obedience to God's Spirit, of course). These are individuals who are not concerned about their pockets, being fully assured that God Almighty is their portion, and Jehovah Jireh is their Provider.

As a matter of fact, for those of us who have received the life-changing truth of Christ, we should make sure we never look at the gospel as being our ticket out of this or that (you tell me) and should not be used to benefit anyone except in bringing glory to God and saving souls from destruction. This pertains to anything we claim we're doing for Christ, and if we constantly check our motives to make sure they're not foul, polluted, tainted, etc. this will definitely help prevent us from being caught up in this dangerous trap.

Please know I'm not saying we can't be prosperous because we can and should be. It's that our prosperity should come from God and not from our own schemes of trying to lay hold of what we think we ought to have.

Proverbs 13:11 in the Amplified version tells us: *"Wealth [not earned but] won in haste or unjustly or from the production of things for vain or detrimental use [such riches] will dwindle away, but he who gathers little by little will increase [his riches]"*. Further, Deuteronomy 8:18 tells us: *"And you shall remember the LORD your God, **for it is He who gives you power to get wealth**, that He may establish His covenant which He swore to your fathers, as it is this day."*

I'm fully aware that 1 Corinthians 9:14 tells us: *"Even so the Lord has commanded that those who preach the gospel should live from the gospel."* This scripture, however, should not be twisted and used as an excuse to manipulate the people of God all because we've got to eat. I say "all because we've got to eat" because I've seen how some artists try to use 1 Corinthians 9:14 as their justification to do many questionable things.

For example, I knew an artist who was really gifted in what he/she did and as a result, just as many have done, quit his/her job. The problem with this is that this particular artist refused to live by anything other than that which they collected from using their gift to preach. However, once their lights, rent, car note, etc. had to be paid, they then went into a complete marketing frenzy by trying to market themselves and sell their products and the gospel. Don't we know the gospel is not for sale? This was all because they feared and thought if they did not get an engagement, they couldn't eat.

Yet, I'm here to tell you when folks are hungry, it can become a very serious thing because you never really know what that person will or will not do as a result of their hunger. Although I'm sure the artist I referred to started out with sincere motives, once the bills started piling up and/or the pride of life started to tell him/her how he/she should be living the "high life" because of being extremely creative and gifted, eventually that which had been pure was contaminated.

Truth is, I write compassionately about this because I've sadly witnessed some artists go into straight depression over not being booked or given a "gig," as some would call it. I have also witnessed some put together honorarium sheets where if they didn't get what they requested, they wouldn't show up and share what God had given them and mandated that they share. If they did, it was done with a nasty attitude like, "Since you don't know my worth, I'll only give a condensed version. I'm not giving or sharing my best." Friend, for those who don't know . . . this is truly a wrong motive. How can we refuse to share what does not belong to us but to God, anyway?

Did you know there are even some artists who are only concerned about getting a lot of numbers so they can make their own name known or great? Well, it's true. People like this are very easy to spot because they are usually very aggressive; they are the ones who constantly stay in the face of others to tell whoever will listen about what all they can do. And so, these are the people I consider to be hungry, hungry for something, but only God knows what. It could be attention, fame, money, etc. Who knows?

However, before I close this chapter what I really wanted to point out is this. If we're in a constant place of expecting to receive, get and have then this is something we absolutely need to check so we can realign ourselves because this attitude does not demonstrate the character of the One we're to exemplify, Jesus. In fact, remember it was Jesus who told us in Acts 20:35 that "...*it is more blessed to give than it is to receive.*" It was our heavenly Father who demonstrated this by "*giving up His only begotten (unique) Son so that whoever believes in (trust in, clings to, relies on) Him shall not perish (come to destruction, be lost) but have eternal (everlasting) life.*" (John 3:16 AMP) He did this because as the beginning of this same passage tells us: "*Our heavenly Father so greatly loved and dearly prized the world...*"

So in short, if our motives are not coming from the perspective of us wanting to do, give, and be a blessing, then once again, we really have to ask ourselves who is making the true profit God or us?

Walk It Out and Focus Questions

> - Meditate on John 3:16 over and over again, and then ask yourself what do you really give up and sacrifice to imitate a portion of the love God has for this world?
> - In Colossians 3:23-24, who are we told that we are serving? How are we told to serve? What does this passage say we will receive as a result? Memorizing this scripture will definitely help you keep your motives straight and not get things twisted.
> - Guard yourself against the secular mentality that tries to make you think somebody owes you something, especially as it pertains to God. The truth is, God doesn't owe us anything. He so graciously gave us salvation, so if anything we owe Him.

Let's Agree in Prayer: *Father, I pray my motives, in all that I do for You, are found pure in Your eyes, and everything I do is done solely for the purpose of Your Kingdom's gain. If or when it is not, I pray You will bring about quick conviction so I may line up according to Your will. Please help me to also stay focused on knowing that as I take care of Your business, You are faithful to take care of mine in whatever way You see fit. In Jesus' name I pray. Amen.*

Chapter 19: Love Them; Don't Condemn Them

Our Approach to the World

Whenever we come into contact with non-believers, it is best that we proceed with extreme caution and give much love not judging or condemning them. Fact is, you never know what a person's background is and the reason why he or she has rejected Christ or haven't yet come to accept Him as Lord and Savior.

On another note, whether we want to accept this or not, many people have been badly bruised, damaged, and hurt by those in the "church". This factor can be contributed to numerous things. A few are due to the hell condemning messages many have preached, pride from those who've felt like they were so much better than them and the actions displayed by believers outside of the church that have been totally in opposition to God's standards. So, because of things like these, unfortunately, some have only been pushed further away from Christ instead of drawing closer.

Believe it or not, there have been some Christians who've gotten into major arguments with non-believers over beliefs to the point you would have thought they were going to straight "duke it out". Others may not have gone to that extreme but have been as loud and obnoxious as they possibly could be in attempting to prove how right they knew they were.
However, this type of behavior totally goes against what the word of God instructs us to do.

Whenever we stand in judgment toward non-believers we're actually killing our opportunity to ever minister to the very ones in whom Christ died for and is in constant intercession for.

2 Timothy 2:23-26 tells us: *"But avoid foolish disputes, knowing that they generate strife, and a servant of the Lord **must not quarrel but be gentle to all**, able to teach, patient, in humility corrects those who are in opposition."* Then this same verse goes on to say: *"**if God perhaps will grant them repentance**, so that they may know the truth, and that they may come to their senses and escape the snare of the devil, having been taken captive by him to do his will."*

So we clearly see from this passage that it's God alone who can grant them repentance. Furthermore, in all sincerity, we should never disrespect non-believers or "put them on blast" all because they haven't yet come to accept the truth of Jesus. Fact is, all of us have been created by God, and the only thing that separates us from them - is grace, grace, grace! The grace of God is still readily available to them, too, because Christ died for us all. Romans 10:13 in the Amplified version tells us: *"For **everyone who calls upon** the name of the Lord [invoking Him as Lord] will be saved."*

Another point to ponder is this, if Christ, Himself, who is the Son of God did not come to condemn the world then who are we to do so?

John 3:17 in the Amplified version tells us: *"For God did not send the Son into the world in order to judge (to reject, to condemn, to pass sentence on) the world, but that the world might find salvation and be made safe and sound through Him."*

Here's something very essential for all of us to reflect on: whenever we stand in condemnation and judgment toward non-believers, we're actually killing our opportunity to ever minister the gospel of Christ to the very ones who Jesus died for and for whom He constantly intercedes. (Hebrews 7:25). Quite frankly, I think if we were to spend more time trying to get into the worlds of those who don't believe, and if they ever communicated to us why it is they don't believe or won't receive Christ as their personal Lord and Savior, I know many of us would be moved with compassion for their souls instead of wanting to "bang the gavel of no mercy".

Personally, I know whenever I'm tempted to judge others, one thing I try to keep in mind is my own daily sin and that I'm in constant need of forgiveness. Also just as God has built my testimony in Him, He is still in the process of building the testimony of others, so once they finally come out of satan's kingdom it'll be forever and not temporary. Heavily considering these two things usually is enough to shift my thinking from judgmental to compassionate.

In all seriousness, I truly believe now is one of the most opportune times for us, collectively as the Body of Christ, to begin sharing and displaying in abundance the true love of Jesus to non-believers. It must be the type of love that Christ lavished upon us while we were yet sinners. Yes, Christ **still** died for us (Romans 5:8). When we do this, they will definitely be able to witness the true authentic love God has for them, instead of feeling as if there's no hope because of our judgment. In these last days, please let's humbly and earnestly embrace this truth. When we love the way Christ loves, we accept. When we judge and condemn, we only reject.

Walk It Out and Focus Questions

> - When tempted to write people off as being "un-savable" or "unusable" for God, a helpful thing to do to keep things in the right perspective is to read and meditate often on the life of Saul who later became known as Paul. Although this apostle was once a persecutor of Christians, he later was converted to a follower of Christ and then used by God to accomplish undeniably great things for His glory.
> - Whenever somebody grieves your spirit to the point they're always on your mind, instead of putting them down with your thoughts and mouth, ask God to give you a heart to pray for them because you never know whether your prayer is the missing key and answer to their deliverance.
> - When you practice keeping your mind stayed upon the redeeming power of Jesus in your own life, you can trust that this will leave very little room for anything else (like judging others) to exist if you remain in constant awe of God's saving power.

➢ What truth does Romans 9:18 reveal to us about God? Please look up this passage to locate the missing words: *"Therefore He has _____ on whom He wills, and whom He wills He _____."*

Let's Agree in Prayer: *Father, I pray all ungodly judgment and condemnation would be removed out of me so absolutely nothing stands in the way of You being able to show Your overwhelming love to those who are in need of it. Help me Lord, to also continuously stay mindful of my past and present sin that, the very reason Your Son came, to seek and save that which was lost (Luke 19:10), can be accomplished. In Jesus' name I pray. Amen.*

Chapter 20: Home Is First

What Does Your Home Look Like?

To those of us who are married whether with or without children, in this chapter I'd like to stress the fact that our families are supposed to be our first ministry. Everything else should follow after that because if those who God has entrusted into our care are not being ministered to by us, then the fact is we are not being good stewards over what God has given us. Granted, I'm not saying we can't have or don't need help with this assignment because Lord knows, getting assistance from others we can trust is almost a must in order to do anything effectively for God. Even with that, we should never solely rely upon the help of others to give our families what we, ourselves, should give them.

Sure, people can come alongside of us and help, but they're not supposed to become us and take our place because it is our assignment. This is why I said our first ministry is supposed to be to those who are in our own home. I'm specifically referring to those who are married with or without children, divorced and/or single with children. However, if you're single without children, this chapter will also greatly benefit you. In reading it, you will gain wisdom you can apply once you are married or to be a blessing by sharing it with others. So, please stay with me.

> **If those in whom, God has entrusted into our care being our family are not being ministered to by us then fact is, we will not have been good stewards over what God gave us.**

Though this is heartbreaking to have to say, I still will. In some instances our homes are beginning to look a lot like the house of Eli. Who was Eli? He was a priest entrusted by God to train up a young boy by the name of Samuel, but when it came to the training up of his own sons, the word of God says: *"Now the sons of Eli were corrupt; **they did not know the Lord**"* (1 Samuel 2:12). In my opinion, I've always found this situation to be quite interesting because their father was a priest. (Please read all about this in 1 Samuel 2-3.). How was it that Samuel, who was under the tutorage of Eli, grew to be so God-fearing but not his sons? I don't know; that's still something I have yet to discover, but one thing this bible truth does reveal to us is if we do not tend effectively to those who are in our homes, the exact same thing could also happen to us as well.

Honestly, this is why if we're really serious about making our homes our first priority, one thing we'll have to do is make sure we guard ourselves against becoming so busy in "ministry" our families rarely see us. There have been too many of us who have already used ministry as an excuse for our absence in our families' lives and many other things. But the word of God has warned us against this by saying: *"But if anyone does not provide for his own, and especially for those of his household, he has denied the faith and is worse than an unbeliever"* (1 Timothy 5:8).

What I'm addressing is the main reason so many marriages of very powerful ministers, singers, actors, rappers, etc. have been wrecked by divorce. Many of them have become very famous, and for some of them it was at the cost of their families because of their neglect. satan can't even be blamed for it. In fact, Mark 3:25 the Amplified version tells us clearly so we will not be deceived that: *"if a house is divided against itself, that house cannot stand."*
Therefore, we should not only allow our families to hear us preach Jesus publicly through whatever it is we do, but most importantly, we should make sure they also witness Jesus being lived out privately in and through our lives at home. When we do this, it will be then and only then that we can truly go forth in the confidence of knowing our home is in order. Our houses must be in order while we are out trying to help and encourage others.

I remember when my husband and I first got married, boy were there those in the church who kept trying to pull us out of the place of rest in which we knew God had us. So one thing we had to quickly realize was that **NO** was also a Holy word especially when something was presented that was against the will of God for us. To others it appeared as if we had fallen off the face of the earth and were just so in love that we decided to forget about God and His work, but the truth is, we realized if we didn't take that time to focus solely on one another in order to build a home together as a couple in Christ, then our disobedience could've resulted in divorce. Looking back, since I've come to understand in a greater way the truth of how *if our home is not tight, nothing else will be right,* I am ever so grateful to God for Him shutting down all my other ministry assignments so I could focus on the most important ministry assignment I'll ever have, my family.

Trust me. Keeping our home first priority is something constant attention must be given to because maintaining family unity is often a constant battle. To be precise, it's a spiritual battle because marriage and family are specific institutions of God that satan and this world would absolutely love to destroy. Hence, in order for it to be successful, not only will we have to work at it, but we will also have to add a whole lot of extra with that work.

I know my prayer for myself has been that I'd be such a good witness of the Lord Jesus in my own home that my witness would actually open the doors of opportunity for me to go forth and share Him with others. I also pray that when I go forth in ministry, I'm celebrated by those in my home and not resented because of my lack of attention to them in any area. So I consistently ask myself this question: "What would it truly matter if I were to gain the whole world, but yet lose my own soul, (the family) God has entrusted into my care?" Selah (meaning to pause and calmly think about what was just said).

I can say with full assurance that ministering love to our families is something we can never do enough of, and so I'd like to challenge you as I challenge myself, to walk out 1 John 3:18 in a much greater way. It reads: *"My little children, let us not love in word or in tongue, but in deed and in truth."*

To the Divorced or Single with Children

Out of the heart of God, I'd like to share a few important pointers with you. First, if you have not been taking care of your children by doing such things like paying child support, spending time with them and the like because you do not want to be bothered, being too busy or not liking your child's mother or father, then these are issues that need to be dealt with and resolved **quickly** because if not, it will definitely affect you and your children later.

Even though you might have to take the humble stance and forgive wrongs that were done to you in order to make the situation right, I can guarantee, in the long run, you'll be able see how doing so will be well worth it. I do understand not every situation is the same, so yours may require a totally different method; however, in the context of what I'm saying, regardless of the method you use, if you've neglected your responsibly to care for your children, you should do everything within your power to change that.

Then after you've done all you know to do to reconcile the situation, if you still don't see any change, it's okay because as long as you have a relationship with the heavenly Father **there is still an abundance of hope** for the situation. Keep the situation lifted up before God in prayer, and allow your faith to be what moves God to answer your request. In the word of God when a man brought his son to Jesus in need of healing, Jesus said to him, "*If you can believe, **all things** are **possible** to him who believes*" (Mark 9:23). Since the word of God in this passage is a 100 percent true, I'd like to encourage you to stir up your faith in God . . . so just as this man witnessed the miraculous, you can also witness the miraculous being done for you.

Walk It Out and Focus Questions

> ➢ If those you live with were to be interviewed and asked whether or not they feel you demonstrate the character of Christ in your home, what do you think their responses would be?
> ➢ Looking at your current situation in your home, do you see any room for improvement where you can take action immediately to let your family know they are first in your life? If so, what would you do?
> ➢ If you are married, try to always honor your spouse by asking them first if it is okay for you to participate in whatever comes your way (even ministry) because by doing this not only will they be fully aware of your itinerary, but this will also make them feel very appreciated by you for taking the time to know and care what they think.
> ➢ Try to involve your family as much as possible in the things you do so they will not feel left out. Also make a habit of scheduling family time where you refuse to allow anything to break your commitment to be with them.

Let's Agree in Prayer: *Father, I pray no matter who I stand before or with that I first minister and care for those in my own home because there is no one greater or closer to my heart than they are, and I want them to know that. I also pray the report my family gives You about me is what allows You to even hear the reports of all others. Please help me to find a place of balance where You, I, and even all those entrusted into my care will not be neglected. In Jesus' name I pray. Amen.*

Chapter 21: Time is of the Essence

Time Can Either Honor or Dishonor Your Name

I don't think anybody has mastered or will ever master or perfect controlling time because there is only One who holds time in His hands. Yet, we do have the ability and responsibility to be accountable to others in the commitments we make to minister the gospel of Jesus Christ through our gifts. Prayerfully, it's something we all are mindful of especially when it comes to showing up on time at the places where we've been invited to share our gifts with believers and non-believers. I say this because whenever somebody invites us to be a part of their event, if we are not in place at the appointed time that can cause disorder. How? As a result of our absence or tardiness, people will be distracted wondering why we're late or MIA (missing in action). And we know that God is a God of order!

We must realize that no matter how anointed we are, if we're always showing up late to our assignments, though people may put up with it for a while, if it continues characteristics and descriptions about us that are not so pleasant or honorable will get attached to our names. Not to mention, repeated tardiness or absenteeism will close many doors of opportunity for us because of these character flaws. Not being on time can dishonor your name. Yet, on the flip side of this, if we're always in position when we're supposed to be, timeliness can bring honor to our names because this shows others that we are dependable and respectful of others' time as well. Please understand the last thing anybody wants to worry about when it's time to execute the vision is where somebody is or whether he or she will show up or not.

> **Whenever someone invites us to be a part of their event if, we are not in place at the appointed time that can cause disorder.**

This is why it's extremely important for us to first count the cost of accepting invitations so that if we commit to do something, we will make the very best effort to also follow through. Actually before we ever commit to do anything, it would really be in our best interest to take all invitations to God in prayer to see whether or not He'd have us to be a part of them. After all, He is the all-knowing One. I mention this because I know how easy it can be to quickly agree to do something over the excitement of being asked and simply having the opportunity to go forth in ministry using our gifts. But, please hear me! If we stay stuck there, unfortunately, focusing too much on the excitement could cause us to miss out on the whole picture and result in great conflict later.

As believers, one thing we must all be extra cautious about is what we speak because as "time is everything" *so is our word*. If we tell someone we're going to do something, we ought to do everything within our power to keep that commitment because if we don't, it may cause the One we say we serve to look bad. For this reason, our word should never be our own word but actually be God's word coming through us. We know everything God says He will do, we can trust Him to do. Since we are supposed to reflect Christ in all we do, we should keep our word, too. If we pray first over our invites, it will prevent us from using our words so casually and being too hasty.

Follow up calls are also very important because they assist us in doing things in the spirit of excellence. Essentially if we commit to do an event, we should also make sure we give those in charge a quick and easy way to be able to contact us at all times if needed. They should not have to make a lot of effort to track us down. This causes frustration. Yet, if we're extremely busy people or slow at returning phone calls, and we are the one who handles all of our ministry affairs, please let those who need to know of your busy schedule so they are aware in advance. This way everybody can be on one accord.

Arrival Time

I'd like to share with you a few benefits of arriving before time to the places you've been invited. When you arrive early…

1. You will have the opportunity to "scout out the land." This means you can check out your environment and be able to pray strategically.
2. You will be able to be informed by God how you will need to navigate in order to complete your assignment.
3. You will be able to affect your atmosphere with Christ, instead of your atmosphere affecting you the way it could if you were to show up late or real close to time.
4. You can be informed about any last minute changes by those in charge so you can adjust accordingly and stay focused without being distracted and stressed out by things that could have been avoided if you had known beforehand.
5. You will be recognized as a person who values your time, and this will cause others to value your time also.
6. You will be able to do what you do for God out of and in peace not having to rush to get in place. I've noticed that people who kind of "go with the flow" or who are always rushing from place to place are a wreck, wrecked with stress. The spirit of busyness is all over them.

Walk It Out and Focus Questions

> If you know you're going to be late to an assignment or just can't make it for whatever reason whether it's an emergency or not, please pick up the phone to advise those who invited you so everything can continue to flow smoothly. From my experiences, I have learned that people really do value communication.
> Whenever invited to do whatever you do for God, try to make sure you always stay within the allotted time you've been given instead of stopping whenever you feel like it. If you don't, you will actually be disrespecting the ones who invited you as well as shaming God's name. If you know in advance you're going to

need more time, it's better to ask for it than just taking it even if you're right in the middle of your presentation.

➢ With TV and radio interviews, always be sure you pay close attention to the person interviewing you. This way you are certain that they're the ones who stay in total control over the interview instead of you. By keeping your eye on the host at all times, you'll be able to pick up on any tips they might be trying to give you during the interview.

➢ Try to arrive everywhere you minister at least 30 minutes before you're scheduled to be there because this will not only help you but will also help others tremendously knowing you're present and in place.

➢ If you know you're one who is always running late to things, ask God to help you in this area. Maybe this could be something you could make a vow unto God to improve on by fasting and being on time to places. I've heard it only takes 30 days to make or break a habit, and so it wouldn't hurt to try this approach.

Let's Agree in Prayer: *Father, I pray I would begin to ponder (study) the path of my feet (Proverbs 4:26) to an even greater extent, so I may follow through with whatever it is I commit to do in the spirit of excellence. I also pray I'll begin to control my time so much so that it brings honor opposed to dishonor to my name or Your name. In Jesus' name I pray. Amen.*

Chapter 22: Open Up!

Allow God to Demonstrate His Love Through You

How we interact with people and how we treat them is a very serious thing to God. I can't possibly count the number of people I've met who've had God's name plastered all over what they do, but they were so nasty in spirit and outright mean, puffed up, or unsociable. Although I can't speak as if I have arrived at flawlessness in this area, I will allow God to minister to me and through me, as I write this chapter. Let's jump right into it!

If God has given us a public ministry and for some reason we have issues with people, meaning we really don't like to have them in our space, then this is something we really do need to be honest with God and ourselves about so we can receive deliverance. Having issues with people or dealing with people is definitely not something we should ever ignore or excuse by saying things like, "That's just me; I've never liked to be around a bunch of people. I don't like to have people in my business, and/or I just don't trust folks because of my past." and so forth. If we do this, we'll be shutting ourselves down from receiving growth in this area, and we definitely don't want to do that since our lives are supposed to be available for Christ in every way because He purchased us with His blood. He says, "feed My sheep." You have to be around the sheep to feed them, and He didn't mean do it with a bad or stand-offish attitude.

> When you're in Christ it's not just about your reputation
> But ultimately
> It's about the reputation of Jesus and how well you represent Him.

Honestly, I can speak about this area in a personal way because I used to have a big issue with allowing people into my space; however, after being around others who had the love of God flowing through them, it didn't take me too long to realize how desperately I needed help. I can remember having a girlfriend, who I'd watch hug and/or say hi to almost everybody she passed by at church. Although many of those times I felt like that was quite extreme, I still knew I needed some of that love.

I was also placed around a minister of the gospel, who I'd watch minister joyfully. He never allowed who he was to prevent him from making sure he showed God's love to all both before and after he ministered. I mean I'd literally watch him go out of his way to meet and greet, and so after being around him and other people like that, I too, couldn't help but desire to walk in a greater level of love toward others.

My process of deliverance in this area however did not begin until I was completely honest with myself and God that I was ready for my walls to come down. Once I did, one of the scriptures God had me meditate on was: "*A man who has friends must himself be friendly...*" (Proverbs 18:24). God also brought to my attention how I had attended a church for over a year but had not met one single person. Of course, this fact further confirmed my need for His help. I knew it was only due to the walls I erected around me and my outward countenance which spoke to others, "Please stay far away from me."

Yet, I can honestly testify that once I was really ready to change, it only took me a week to meet over 70 people at my church. I can remember the number so vividly because I counted every single person. I was so excited to have finally met others. Truly, that was the start of my new day.

Even though I made great strides to open up after that, I still noticed once I got heavily involved in the ministry it was still an area where God had to deal with me. Sadly, whenever somebody would speak if I didn't know them, I didn't respond. It wasn't because I didn't want to, but mainly I'd be wondering if or how they really knew me. I'd spend so much time racking my brain over the "how they knew me" and "why the person spoke," that guess what? By the time I was finished, they'd be gone. They'd be gone with an impression about me which I'm sure was only disappointing, misunderstood and not positive in any way.

Finally, one day when I was sensitive enough to hear God's voice, I basically heard Him say, "Stop wasting time on the "who's, what's, when's, where's, why's, and how's," just speak to show my love because it really doesn't matter whether they know you or not." After I received that insight, from that point on, I'd smile and speak joyfully to everyone knowing that at least when they left my presence they would do so with a positive impression about me instead of a negative one.

In fact, speaking about impressions, I know you've heard this said time and time again. I'd still like to say it just once more in order to stress the importance and truth in knowing that *first impressions really do mean everything* especially when you're an ambassador for Christ. One thing we have to always be mindful of is that we never know who it is God will allow us to meet and/or cross our path. This is why I believe His word tells us in Hebrews: 13:2 "***Do not forget to entertain strangers***, *for by so doing some people have **entertained angels** without knowing it*."

Remember once you're put in the public's eye, many of the people who will speak to you will actually be your supporters. Believe me; they're the last ones you want to disrespect, "dog out", or snub all because you do not feel like being bothered or whatever the case may be. We all have challenges and what some may call bad days, but if we're constantly having them then that's our clue we need to quickly get with our heavenly Father so He can reveal to us what's going on. Listen to me! *When you're in Christ, it's not just about your reputation but ultimately about the reputation of Christ and how well you represent Him.*

Romans 12:13 tells us we are to be "*given to hospitality*" and (Colossians 3:12 NIV) tells us to: "*clothe ourselves with compassion, kindness, humility, gentleness and patience.*" In short, we must refuse to allow our flesh, personalities, and past experiences to prevent us from extending the love of God to others. We must do with all genuineness what I stated in the subtitle; allow God's love to be demonstrated through us.

Walk It Out and Focus Questions

- ➢ Try to make a habit of reflecting on every assignment you complete and analyze how well you did or did not do in stretching outside of your comfort zone to be sociable and open up to others. Make it your aim to be accessible to the people to whom you minister.
- ➢ Since eye contact has been proven to make people feel as if you really take interest in them and are speaking to them directly, try to practice making eye contact with all the people with whom you come into contact.
- ➢ Always be aware of what your body language and posture are saying to others because our body has a language of its own.
- ➢ If you compare your fruit to the fruit of the Spirit found in (Galatians 5:22-23) on a regular basis, you will be able to see how much love, joy, peace, long suffering, faithfulness, gentleness, goodness, kindness, and self-control you really have.

Let's Agree in Prayer: *Lord, since You and Your Kingdom are at hand, please help me to die more and more to myself so I may open up in a greater way to truly show forth Your authentic love to others. Help me to always keep in the forefront of my mind that it is not about me and how I may feel, but it is all about You and how I present You to others. In Jesus' name I pray. Amen.*

Chapter 23: Our Attire Matters

Are We Clothed Rightly or Worldly?

Whenever we are front and center before God's people, please be aware that what we wear really does matter. Since we live in a day and age where anything goes, particularly as it pertains to our clothing, we truly have to be extra cautious about what we allow ourselves to wear because what may be hip or appropriate for our culture may in fact be outright offensive and worldly to God. Hence, the question, "Are we clothed rightly or worldly?"

Let me expound a little further on exactly what I mean by sharing a few things I have witnessed some artists wear, but while I do please keep in mind that these individuals were placed in a position to minister to God's people.

At one event I was hosting, some men with integrity told me how there was a sister on stage who didn't have a bra on underneath her shirt, and when I questioned how they knew, both of the men stated they could see things they shouldn't be able to see if she had on one. At another event I saw a guy jumping all around on the pulpit with his pants sagging so low I could see his bottom and although he did have shorts on underneath. For all I know, they could've been his boxers. Whether it was or was not his underwear, his bottom showing was very obvious to both me and others. At another event I saw a sister who was very top heavy wearing a skin tight t-shirt with lace all over the front of it, but what really made it so eye-catching was when she jumped around so did her chest.

> **When I ask God for His opinion about what I should wear, I notice my search for an appropriate outfit becomes much easier and my look much more becoming and tasteful.**

Unfortunately, though I hate to even say this, I've seen some of our most seasoned Christian artists exposing too much of their flesh and particularly things like cleavage. As a matter of fact, for many, who minister in one way or the other, this has almost become completely acceptable. I shared a few of the things I've witnessed to help you identify with where I'm coming from when I say, "Our attire matters!"

Now, let me stop to talk about myself in this area for a moment because in my past I've found myself saying on numerous occasions, "Well, at least I don't look like this or that." referring to what I've seen others wear in the world and in the church as a way to excuse my attire. I also have compared my current style of dressing at times with how I previously dressed when I was of the world by saying things like "Well, at least I'm not showing my belly, skin, etc." However, it didn't take me too long to realize that if I continued to compare my look and clothing by the world's standards, although I might not show this or that, it could still have me going forth ending up looking like a complete well, let's just say "hoochie."

This is why I humbly confess that after missing the mark time and time again, I now constantly ask God, "Okay Lord, what do you want me to wear? Is this okay? Is this too short or too tight? Are any body parts being exposed or highlighted, etc?" Why? We live in a world that's full of nothing but sexual and sensual implications that are not appropriate when ministering the gospel of Jesus Christ. It may be fine in the world's eye, and/or okay in the church because the majority of Christians have accepted worldly dressing styles, but it still may not be at all acceptable to God. So, personally I've noticed when I ask God for His opinion about what I should or should not wear, my search for an appropriate outfit becomes a lot easier and my look much more becoming and tasteful.

Now I know a lot of times even when it comes to our clothing we may say things like, "I'm just trying to relate." Though I can understand wanting to relate, I cannot understand when our method of relating ends up diluting and/or contaminating the message of the gospel. We can relate, but we do not have to lose our integrity as a whole while trying to do so.

Here's something else that's very key for all of us to keep in mind and that is that the spirit of lust not only rules in the world but also now rules heavily in the church. You may think there's no harm being done when you wear certain types of clothing, feeling as if you have been freed up in this area, but the truth is a lot of our sisters and brothers in Christ have not. Therefore, because of this, we really ought to do all we can in order to assist them in their process of deliverance since we are supposed to be our brothers' and sisters' keeper, if you know what I mean.

Please do not misunderstand me because in no way am I'm saying that we cannot have "spice" and "flavor" when it comes to our dress because we most definitely can; however, what I am suggesting is that we should be certain that what we wear glorifies God and does not offend Him.

In this chapter, for the "Walk It Out" section, which you are about to read, I'd like to bring to your attention that I intentionally tailored it for the men and for the women separately. I did so because I wanted to speak to each gender privately. So if you would, please respectfully only read the section that pertains to you. Also, for the *Let's Agree in Prayer* section, everybody should participate in reading that portion before going on to the next chapter.

Walk It Out and Focus Questions

To Ladies Only

Walk It Out and Focus Questions

To Ladies Only

- Ladies, if you have curves, please be sure whatever you wear compliments your body instead of highlighting the different parts of your body. For example, if you can see the dimples in your thighs or your panty line shows through your pants, those are clear indications what you're wearing is too tight.
- If you like to wear "low riders," the cut of jeans that are in style today, please just make sure your entire bottom is covered up both when you're standing and sitting to prevent being exposed.
- Ladies, also note that you can always wear body suits, spandex, or stockings underneath your clothes as a way to hide your panty line and skin. You also can double up on shirts if need be to hide your bra straps and/or bra from showing through your clothes. If you're one who likes to wear thongs, this is something **YOU ALONE** should know you have on. Be sure that in no way is it exposed to others when you bend, sit, and stand.
- If you know in advance you'll be moving around all over the place, or just in case you might be, it's always best to wear extra support with such things like supportive bras, girdles, slips, etc. to assist in keeping your body parts secure and in place.
- If you're top heavy and showing your cleavage is something you've never really paid close attention to for whatever reason, out of the love of Christ for you, I'd like you to know that showing your cleavage is a huge distraction. You may feel as if it's okay because you've already covered up the majority of your chest, but please be made aware that it's the minority that still causes the distraction.
- One way to tell if what you're wearing is cut too low is by checking this: if you can see the top part of your breasts coming out of the top part of your shirt or you can see the beginning point to the crease in between your breasts then your dress or shirt is cut too low. Many shirts nowadays are made low-cut, but ladies this is where we will have to get creative by doubling up and or not wearing the shirt or dress at all in order to stay decent.
- Please also note if you have background singers, musicians, dancers, hype people, etc., it is also extremely important for you to pay close attention to what they are wearing as well because not only do they represent you, but most importantly our heavenly Father.

Walk It Out and Focus Questions

<u>To Men Only</u>

Walk It Out and Focus Questions

<u>To Men Only</u>

- ➤ If you're one who likes to wear baggy pants, please make sure they're not so low people can see your bottom or shorts. This also applies to when you are jumping around.
- ➤ For those of you who like to wear the skin tight muscle shirts, tank tops, tight white t-shirts, please know though they are cute, unfortunately, they can without a doubt cause unwanted aroused emotions in both men and women as a result of them being worn.
- ➤ Even dress shirts if unbuttoned too low can be a huge distraction. If the individual begins to sweat, the wet look can display a totally different look than what I'm sure was originally intended.
- ➤ To those who like to get dressed to "the nines" and wear things like pinstriped suits, hats to the side, gator shoes, etc., to stay brief on this subject, there's a big difference between getting dressed looking sharp and getting dressed looking like you are some kind of gangster or pimp with an attitude attached to you like, "I'm the man," or "I'm running this show." When you get dressed up, make sure there's no other spirit attached to you other than the Spirit of the living God.
- ➤ Please also note if you have background singers, musicians, dancers, hype people, etc., it is also extremely important for you to pay close attention to what they are wearing as well because not only do they represent you, but most importantly our heavenly Father.

Let's Agree in Prayer

Let's Agree in Prayer: *Father, please help me to show forth Your glory in even my attire by being very selective as to what I allow myself to wear. Also, help me to include You in this process so I may rely upon Your wisdom instead of just following the trends and wisdom of this world. In Jesus' name I pray. Amen.*

Chapter 24: Role Models

Our Actions Count

One of the number one things we hear a lot of now days pertaining to entertainers is the all too common saying "I'm not a role model." The main reason people say this is because many do not want to own up and take any responsibility or be held accountable for their actions so they'll use that excuse. On the flip side of this, for those of us who are in the Christian community, some of the things you'll hear us say are "I'm not perfect; I'm only human, and that's just me," and the like. Which to a large degree is almost the same thing as saying, "I'm not responsible."

However, one day when I was really meditating on this whole role model thing, I came to understand that if we do anything for God, being a role model is not an option but a **mandate**. What I mean is we're not only supposed to be responsible to God for our actions but also responsible to others making sure we go the extra mile *on purpose* to represent God well in all facets of our ministries and lives. Now I do recognize that none of us are perfect, yet we should still be at least striving to be more like Christ instead of using excuses like the ones I mentioned previously.

> **For those of us who do anything for God, being a role model is not an option but a mandate.**

Also, while I continued to meditate on being a role model, God started to impress upon my heart how He's not just looking for role models, but He's actually looking for "whole models." These are people who have been made complete in Him, by Him, and are not dependent on anyone or anything else except Him.

To take it a step further, God revealed to me how He not only desires for us to be role and whole models but ultimately holy models. These are individuals who are set apart for His use. I'll definitely discuss this in more detail in the chapter entitled, *"God Is Calling Us to Be Holy (Set Apart)."* In general, can you see the escalation in what I'm saying? Beyond a shadow of a doubt, it is God's will for us to be constantly progressing in our walk with Him and not become stagnate, regress and/or get sidetracked. We can walk in God's will for us if we set out to intentionally and continually place ourselves in a position to receive God's deliverance for our lives. Deliverance means release, liberation, relief and freedom from everything and anything that has or has had us bound.

Despite the fact that deliverance has been looked upon by some as being something spooky, I have to tell you there is nothing spooky about being transformed into the very image of God's Son. Since deliverance is the way to achieve this, it should be welcomed. In fact, I'd like to share something God shared with me about being delivered. Before I do, let me explain to you why I even needed the revelation. I needed it because, honestly, in the past I frequently had pity parties whenever it was my time to experience a greater level of God's deliverance. I'd feel like, "Man, here we go again." I'd also think, "What's the use of God even using me at all since I'm such a work?" But this is where God stepped in and revealed to me that as long as I continued to allow myself to receive deliverance then I was actually right on point. Deliverance is the key to total transformation.

After I finally came to grips with the fact that I should essentially constantly be under construction, what I once cringed at because I didn't have a true understanding of the purpose or process, I'm now able to embrace. I count it an honor that God would even allow me to go through each and every process of deliverance. Indeed the process can be very painful at times, but I still have come to appreciate it because I notice once He's finished in an area, I'm much freer and able to give Him greater glory. I like the way Hebrews 12:11 says it: *"Now no chastening seems to be joyful for the present, but painful; nevertheless, afterward it yields the peaceable fruit of righteousness to those who have been trained by it."*

You may have noticed how I repeated over and over that we need to **receive our deliverance.** Well, I did so because I really wanted to stress the fact that God will approach us at different times about different things. When He does, we are the ones who have to open ourselves up to Him to receive it. This process also requires obedience to His instructions so we can then be delivered.

Essentially, I've always associated God's deliverance process with the "cleaning of a house" because in order to do so and be effective, you normally will only do one room at a time. Depending on the work involved in the project, it may take days, weeks, months or even years before it's completed. Because of God's amazing power, compassion, and understanding of how much we can handle at one time, He usually delivers us in stages as well.

I close with a word of encouragement to both you and myself as we continue to receive our deliverance from the hand of God. That word is: *"…We can be confident of this very thing that He who has begun a good work in us shall complete it till the day of Jesus Christ"* (Philippians 1:6). So with that being said, let's hold on to this liberating truth while making sure we take greater responsibility in not only becoming the role, whole but also ultimately becoming the holy models in which God seeks.

Walk It Out and Focus Questions

> ➢ One thing you can do in order to make sure you stay sensitive to God's delivering work in your life is to constantly ask questions like, "Okay God, what area (room) are you working on me in now? How's it going? Are you receiving the results You set out to receive?" Other internal spirit to spirit questions should be asked because by doing so, you will actually be walking out what (1 Corinthians 11:32) has encouraged us to do, which is to judge ourselves that we are not condemned with this world.

> To locate the missing words of this passage, please look up Proverbs 3:12. It reads: *"For whom the LORD loves He _____, Just as a father the son in whom he delights."* And Hebrews 12:6 says: *"For whom the LORD loves He _____, and scourges every son whom He receives."*
> Would you agree that by knowing these scriptures persevering through [God's] process of deliverance will be a little easier?

Let's Agree in Prayer: *Lord, make my goal to model Your character in such a way that others also will desire to imitate You. And help me, Lord, to take full responsibility for all of my actions while continuing to check them until they finally line up with Your will. In Jesus' name I pray. Amen.*

Chapter 25: God Is Calling Us to Be Holy

(Set Apart)

Hold Yourself Accountable

For those of us who've accepted Jesus as our personal Lord and Savior, we have been called to live holy. This simply means to live a "set apart" lifestyle for God's glory. Because, God has paid a high price for us with the precious blood of Jesus, His Son, we should live as though our lives belong to Him. They do!

2 Corinthians 5:15 in the Amplified version tells us: *"And He died for all, so that all those who live might live no longer to and for themselves, but to and for Him who died and was raised again for their sake."*

God has expressed His desire for us to be holy so many times throughout His word that it is absolutely astounding. One occasion is found in Leviticus 11:45, where it says: *"For I am the LORD who brings you up out of the land of Egypt, to be your God. **You shall therefore be holy**, for I am holy."*

If you know you're in need of desperate deliverance due to continual sin being in your life, then please for the benefit of your soul do not hesitate to just sit yourself down in ministry.

Although God desires us to be holy but already knows that holiness is not something we could ever accomplish in our own strength, He allows His Holy Spirit to be given to those who've accepted His Son's death, burial, and resurrection. We have the Holy Spirit's divine assistance and enablement to help us execute the Father's will, which is to be holy.

Furthermore, Ephesians 4:21-24 in the Amplified version tells us: *"Assuming that you have really heard Him and been taught by Him, as [all] Truth is in Jesus [embodied and personified in Him], **Strip yourselves of your former nature** [put off and discard your old unrenewed self] which characterized your previous manner of life and becomes corrupt through lusts and desires that spring from delusion; **And be constantly renewed in the spirit of your mind** [having a fresh mental and spiritual attitude], And **put on the new nature** (the regenerate self) **created in God's image,** [Godlike] **in true righteousness and holiness."** This is not always an easy thing to do, but we still must keep in mind this truth: **to whom much is given, much is required** (Luke 12:48), and know God would never call us to do something if He didn't, first, enable us to do it.

We should no longer tolerate sin, neither ours nor others'. That's right! Instead, we must begin to look at sin with the same level of seriousness and gravity as God does. The reason I say this is because I believe if we were do so, we wouldn't see so much of the mess we've all witnessed as of late taking place within the church.

Have you ever sincerely wondered how it is that so much sin is accepted and obvious in the lives of some Christian artists we see today? Well, I have, and when I inquired of the Lord why, He revealed to me that it is largely due to many refusing to have any true accountability placed around them.

Honestly, there are some artists, who have entirely too many buddies placed around them and not enough prophets who won't excuse their "mess". We need prophets (mentors) like Nathan was to David (Please read 2 Samuel, 11-12.). Even with mature mentors around us, it is still our own personal responsibility to make sure we reach the point of maturity where we say, mean, and live in a way that even if nobody ever knows what's going on with us behind closed doors, we still will not entertain sin. Why is this important? We must all do what (Philippians 2:12) instructs us to do, *"Work out our own salvation with fear and trembling."*

Let me talk to you specifically about sin for a minute. Did you know there was a time that if one in ministry was caught in sin, they'd be required to sit down for an extended amount of time? Well it's true, and it wasn't until that person received extensive counseling and deliverance that they would be allowed to return to his or her position. However, nowadays, many do not have that type of real accountability. We have situations where some artists are continuing to sin habitually and think nothing of it. It doesn't bother them at all. This reminds me of what 1 Timothy 4:2 says concerning some having their consciences seared and have become liars and hypocrites compromising their faith. Then for the few who may have been caught in blatant, open sin recently, it was treated like it was something minor and inconsequential, if it was mentioned at all.

If what I just spoke about has been you and/or if you ever find yourself in this type of situation where you know you're in need of desperate help and deliverance because of continual sin in your life, then please do not EVER hesitate to just "**SIT YOURSELF DOWN IN MINISTRY.**" Why? By doing so, you'll be taking authority and walking in victory over those demonic spirits that have tried to control you, and most importantly, saving your soul from eternal destruction.

See, one of the biggest lies the devil tries to make those who are in this situation believe is that the people of God cannot do without their ministry during a time of much needed deliverance. But the devil is a liar! Please… hear me. If the ones you sit under or minister to are truly people of God, then they'll appreciate your honesty and integrity. They'll wait for you to come forth as pure gold. Above all else, what ultimately matters here is that you will have the true freedom and peace of knowing you're making your heavenly Father proud by refusing to entertain such things like, adultery, fornication, uncleanness, lewdness, idolatry, sorcery, hatred, contentions, jealousies, outbursts of wrath, selfish ambitions, dissensions, heresies, envy, murders, drunkenness, revelries, and the such abominations found in Galatians 5:19-21. We've been told in 2 Corinthians 5:10: *"For we must all appear before the judgment seat of Christ, that each one may receive the things done in the body, according to what he has done, whether good or bad."*

In closing, I'd like for us to ponder what Paul said in 1 Corinthians 9:27 because this is such a key component in helping us hold ourselves accountable. Paul said: "***But I discipline my body and bring it into subjection***, *lest when I have preached to others, I myself should be disqualified.*" Paul also stated in a few verses before that: "*Do you not know that those who run in a race all run, but one receives the prize?" Therefore Paul says, "Run in such a way that you may obtain it*" (1 Corinthians 9:24). And so, by disciplining our bodies, bringing it into subjection and running the race with similar fervency as to receive the prize, this helps us answer the call of God to live out the "set apart" (holy) way. Let's embrace these precious weighty words spoken by Paul as our very own that we may also receive the crown of victory, which Paul said he knew was laid up in heaven for him (2 Timothy 4:8).

Walk It Out and Focus Questions

- ➢ **Examine yourself often**. Make it a holy habit. Have time with God on a regular basis where you get high in the spirit realm in order to see what God sees as it pertains to your everyday living. Then begin to eliminate those things you know do not please Him.
- ➢ **Accept Godly rebuke**. Learn to value it, both from God and others because if you don't, you will only hinder yourself and could possibly be setting yourself up to be turned over to a debase mind or destruction.
- ➢ **Purify yourself**. Some things God will do for us, but there are many things God wants us to learn how to do for ourselves by simply using the common sense, wisdom and Holy Spirit He's already given us. What does Colossians 3:5-10 tell us?
- ➢ **Meditate and confess**. The truth is that you are not your own, having been bought with the very blood of Jesus. 1 Corinthians 6:19-20 is a great passage of scripture to meditate on until you actually begin to see yourself walking in a more circumspect way. It reads*: "Or do you not know that your body is the temple of the Holy Spirit who is in you, whom you have from God, and you are not your own? For you were bought at a price; therefore glorify God in your body and in your spirit, which are God's.*"
- ➢ **Fast**. This is a big one! Fasting means to initiate death to your flesh by denying yourself both good and bad things (my definition). Start taking notice of the things you like to do or feel like you can't do without, and then offer things like that up to God as a means of sacrifice. Remember, since God knows your heart, He'll know what a sacrifice is for you regardless of how big or small it may appear to you and others.

Let's Agree in Prayer: *Father, I pray during my stay here on earth, I will live in such a way that demonstrates to all that I do reverence You. Please help me to answer Your call to be "set apart" in a greater way since living in holiness without spot or blemish is ultimately Your will for my life. In Jesus' name I pray. Amen.*

Chapter 26: There's Suppose to Be a Difference

Light Versus Darkness

Most definitely there is supposed to be a difference between those of us who are the children of God and those who are only His creation but still under the influence of the devil. Not only that, but there should also be a definitive distinction between those who just claim the name of Christ in church yet refuse to live out His life through obedience to His will.

In all simplicity, what I mean here is; having made Jesus Lord over our lives, we ought to have experienced an evident, obvious, apparent, clear, and unmistakable outward change. Yes, a magnificent change that has taken place on the inside of us that is so amazing that it cannot help overflowing into outward manifestations. It should be such a great change that is not demonstrated "here and there" but on a continual basis. Not only should we recognize this change in ourselves, but others should witness this change and be able to testify to the differences in us as well.

> **As a result to us Having made Jesus Lord over our lives We ought to have experienced an evident, obvious, apparent, clear, and unmistakable inward change that is reflected outwardly.**

Moreover, since we're told in 2 Corinthians 5:17: "Therefore, *if anyone is in Christ, he is a **new creation**; old things have passed away; behold **all things** have become new,*" I believe if we have truly experienced this conversion, it should be reflected in all we do. This is inclusive of but not limited to the way we walk, the way we talk, our demeanor, personality, the way we carry ourselves, dress and the list continues on and on and on.

On the flip side of true Holy Spirit transformations, whenever there's a person who lives a life of habitual sin, sooner or later you will know. How? The word of God tells us sin leads to death (Romans 6:23). This death is not only something that takes place inwardly but also outwardly to the point that eventually you will even see this death displayed on a person's countenance.

Case in point, by doing what I do, I've had the chance to glance at many different pictures taken by Christian artists including models, rappers, actors, singers, and others. Sadly, I have noticed how some of the photos honestly looked like the pictures I took when I was in the clubs. Some of the shots I saw undeniably had the spirit of lust all over them.

As a matter of fact, while I'm speaking about pictures let me ask, you know how we've all been told that "a picture is worth a thousand words," if someone were to stop and take a look at one of your pictures today, what would they see? What would your picture tell them about you? I ask this soul-searching question because some of us have tried so hard to relate to the world. Unfortunately, we've ended up looking like dope boys, pimps, gangsters and thugs. Ladies, some of us look like hoochie mamas, or very masculine instead of being soft, feminine, and virtuous. Why is this? Simply put, there has not yet been a total change as described in 2 Corinthians 5:17.

If you didn't know this, it is God's utmost desire to transform all of us in such a way that everything about us is *radically* changed. This is why the time has come for all of us to answer God's call and go to another level of being set apart for His glory because if we don't, I can guarantee you that God will expose those who've been living double lives, one of sin and masked by hypocrisy.

Furthermore, I'd like to point something else out. Did you know that part of the reason why some non-believers have steered far away from Jesus is because of what they've seen some of us who say we're Christians do and represent? If the truth were to really be told, when some of them have glanced at those of us in the gospel industry, in some instances, they have not been able to see any difference between themselves and us whatsoever. As a result of seeing us act like they do, wearing the same clothing, dancing the same dances, singing the same lyrics, using the same beats or outright stealing theirs, the famous saying, "*And they call themselves a Christian*," lives on.

The fact is God's word tells us we are being transformed into the very image of His Son; therefore, it would be very wise and favorable for us to yield to this transformation process, while going after God until the level of change He desires becomes evident. This change must be so evident that we not only notice but others who come into contact with us will desire to change because we have the Spirit of the living God living inside of us.

Finally, let's reflect on a few scriptures that exhort us to live in the light. In John 12:46 Jesus said: "*I have come as a **light** into the world, that whoever believes in Me **should not abide in darkness**.*"

Romans 13:12 tells us: "*The night is far spent, the day is at hand. Therefore let us cast off the works of darkness, and let us put on the armor of **light**.*"

And Ephesians 5:8 reads: "*For you were once darkness, but now you are **light** in the Lord. Walk as children of **light**.*"

Walk It Out and Focus Questions

> ➢ What changes, if any, do you know beyond a shadow of a doubt have taken place in you since you've accepted Jesus into your life?
> ➢ If you were to look at a picture of yourself before and after your walk in Christ began, would you see a difference between the two?
> ➢ What changes, if any, are you currently witnessing take place in your walk with God?

Let's Agree in Prayer: *Father, I pray when others look at me, whether they know me or not, they will still be able to identify me as being a child of Yours. I also pray my changes in some way, shape or form is evident to others by having yielded and continuously yielding to your transforming work in my life. In Jesus' name I pray. Amen.*

Chapter 27: Out of the Abundance of the Heart

Monitor Your Flow

If you ever want to know what's in a person's heart, all you have to do is simply pay close attention to what comes out of him or her because eventually that will tell you what's truly in their hearts. Matthew 12:34-35 confirms this by saying: "…*For out of the abundance of the heart the mouth speaks. A good man out of the good treasure of his heart brings forth good things, and an evil man out of the evil treasure brings forth evil things.*"

In the same way, it's also very easy to know what a person may watch a lot on TV, listen to, and the kind of company he or she may keep since this also will be displayed in and through them. For as the saying goes, "What goes in must come out, and what comes out is what surrounds us." This is why there's so much truth to 1 Corinthians 15:33 which says: "***Do not be deceived evil company corrupts good habits.***"

In fact, as you can always tell what an artist sees by their artwork, what a writer feels by what they write, what a singer, rapper, poet, and spoken word artist are filled with by what they speak. You can also tell the level of one's purification by simply observing whatever a person exhibits.

> **If you ever want to know what's in a person's heart, all you have to do is pay close attention to what comes out of them and that will reveal their heart.**

To bring the topic "out of the abundance of the heart, the mouth speaks" a little further home, I'd like to give you an example. Having done radio for quite some time, I've heard a lot of different types of gospel music. Honestly, some of it grieved my spirit to the point that I quickly had to turn it off. Why? Out of the abundance of their heart they spoke, and some of what I heard was no different than what I once listened to in the secular arena. Meaning, I still heard a lot of competition, boasting in self, lust for material things, and the artist's talent being exalted instead of God. There was profanity every once in awhile, and surprisingly, I even heard some artists boast in their salvation as if they obtained it all on their own. Yet, we all know the truth about that.

Anyway, getting back to the music I heard, although some of it was contrary to the very character of God, I never felt as if these people didn't know God. It was just obvious to me that they had not yet come into a deeper relationship with God or received a deeper revelation of God because their abundance proved it. Though some of the music may have had a nice beat, and the artists had a nice appearance, other than that, it was still quite empty of the true Spirit of God. The word of God tells us: "*If any man speak let him speak the oracles of God if any man minister, let him do it as with the ability which God supplies, **that in all things God may be***

glorified through Jesus Christ*, to whom belong the glory and the dominion forever and ever Amen"* (1 Peter 4:11).

See as artists (ministers) of Jesus Christ, one thing we must know is that we're the ones held responsible for making sure we purify the gifts and talents we've been given so they can be used for the glory of God. One way we can do that is by refusing to allow ourselves to be entertained by things that are abominable to God. What I mean is we have to get to a place and stay in a place where we make it a habit to scrutinize everything before allowing it to enter into us. Personally, I think Ephesians 5:15-16 says it best telling us: *"See then that you walk **circumspectly***, *not as fools but as wise, redeeming the time, because the days are evil."*

Let me share with you a personal example demonstrating what I mean when I say we should scrutinize everything. When I was told by God He was going to use me in the music industry, I knew in order for Him to do so I first had to release the old so I could receive the new. That meant I had to completely separate myself from secular music altogether because at that time all I knew was how to rap about money, myself, and material belongings.

Since music had such an impact on me, when I did try to listen to secular music on occasion, I found myself trying to rap for God but still sounding like those in the world instead of being original. By finally cutting out secular music altogether, I was purifying my talent for God's use solely. I can testify to the immense difference it has made not only in my music but, most importantly, in every area of my life.

Proverbs 18:21 tells us: *"Death and life are in the power of the tongue and those who love it will eat of its fruit."*

Matthew 12:36-37 warns us by saying: *"But indeed I say to you that for every idle word men speak they will give account of it in the Day of Judgment. For by your words you will be justified and by your words you will be condemned."*

These particular scriptures deal directly with what we are talking about in this chapter, what we speak, but they can also be applied to what we do.

My main purpose for writing this chapter was to encourage all of us to sincerely and truthfully analyze, monitor, and examine thoroughly what it is that comes out of us. We must be certain whether or not our words and actions are helping or hindering those who've been entrusted into our care. I know I referred quite a bit to music in this chapter, but know that was only one point of reference; the chapter as a whole was written to be inclusive of all creative forms of expression.

Walk It Out and Focus Questions

> ➤ For at least two weeks intentionally analyze what your "abundance" is. You can do this by annotating everything you allow to be deposited into you during that time. This will include things like annotating what types of programs you watch on TV, radio stations you listen to, websites you visit, entertainment you engage

in, and even your friendships and who you consider a friend and what you do with them. After the two weeks are up, you should be able to have a pretty good idea about what your abundance is by looking at your list because whatever is in us will be what comes out of us.

➢ Once you have your list, ask yourself this question: Is my path filled with the light of Jesus Christ or is it filled with darkness? And if you notice anything you'd like to change or God is leading you to change, share that with somebody else who can hold you accountable in your commitment.

Let's Agree in Prayer: *Father, I pray my abundance would be what is truly pleasing in your sight, and I never give anything contaminated to Your people due to my intake. I pray in all I do I will begin to ask myself this question, "Is this or that feeding life or death into me?" And if it's feeding me death, I pray for Your strength, Lord, to disconnect so I may be a set apart vessel for Your use. In Jesus' name I pray. Amen.*

Chapter 28: Let's Talk Submission

Are You Covered?

Submission is a word that really puts people on the edge of their seats both those who are in Christ and those who are not. Why? Mainly because of the way it's been portrayed and explained to some. For many, submission has been misused and misunderstood as a form of manipulation or domination over another. However, when I speak about the word submission, I'm talking about *God's original intent* where if carried out in its proper order will effectively help position those who are submitted to receive God's unlimited blessings.

However, submission is something this world absolutely hates and rightfully so because the world's ways are totally opposite to the ways of God. (Please read 1 Corinthians 2:14). Unfortunately, there are also many believers who are not in favor of submission either. The reality is that submission should be thoroughly embraced because it was originated by God, Himself.

Regardless of what we call them, there ought to be somebody somewhere who can attest to the fact that we are without doubt a submitted vessel of God.

Although I acknowledge the fact we live in a system that teaches us we don't have to answer to anybody for anything, and we're our own man or woman, to submit can be a very hard thing to carry out. However, if we really want to do things God's way not ours or the devil's, then we'll have to go against that system and know when it comes to living out the set apart way, SUBMISSION is the key.

As I mentioned before, even Jesus, Himself, was under extreme submission to God, the Father, and took no credit whatsoever for anything He did but boldly proclaimed how He only did what He saw His father do (See John 5:19.). He made sure everybody was fully aware that He did not operate out of His own authority but was submitted to His Father. With that being said, I'd like for us to ask ourselves: "In whose authority do we operate out of?" Are we also submitted to the Father as Jesus was?" I ask this because if not, unfortunately, we are setting ourselves up for a rude awakening.

In fact, it is very crucial for us to be submitted to our heavenly Father. I also believe it's just as important for us to be submitted to those on earth who are submitted to God's will. Whether we call them an elder, pastor, teacher, prophet, prophetess, reverend, mother or father in the faith, apostle, Dr., mentor, minister, sister, brother, bishop or some other title, we ought to be fully submitted to someone somewhere who can readily attest to the truth that we are called by God and a submitted vessel of God.

Why? When we are, it is not only positioning us to receive God's unlimited blessings, but it is also helping to keep us from becoming prideful, thinking we don't need anyone else's help. We all need somebody! Most importantly, when we're submitted, we will also have accountability, and this will help us to keep our minds focused on prayerfully doing the will of God.

Another wonderful benefit of being submitted (i.e., covered) is that while you're out doing the work of the ministry, you'll have an abundance of prayers being sent up to heaven on your behalf. Prayer is something we can **never** have enough of because it's vitally necessary in order to be effective. Regrettably, I can't possibly list all the benefits of being submitted because of the limited space I have; however, I still pray you've been able to see its significance.

Actually, out of a strong desire to see restoration be brought about in whatever areas it is needed, I will highlight a few reasons why some artists have been closed-minded and turned off to being submitted. Let's take a look.

Hurt is a big reason that keeps so many people un-submitted because of past circumstances and situations that may have caused them too much pain. Though this may be true, here's a secret in order to help all who've been offended or hurt. The secret is that the pain you experienced may have only been a direct set up and attack from satan, for the purpose of trying to move you out of your God-given position and, if possible, into a place where you would have a stone-cold heart toward those in authority. Why? In reality, even satan knows about the power of being submitted. This is why even in our pain, we have to be set like flint, unmovable and only dependent on God to release us from the source of hurt. He will work from the root. If we don't, we will potentially fall into satan's trap, thus the reason why it is truly a necessity for us to receive our healing and deliverance so we can "keep on keepin' on" in Jesus' name.

Lack of recognition is another reason why some artists will not submit because they feel like they're not receiving any attention from their pastors, elders, leaders, and /or teachers, etc. Because of this, they'll say things like, "I don't fit in anywhere, and/or no one recognizes my gifts and talents." To those in this category, although I've mentioned this before, it's worth saying again, in our walk with God there may be times when He'll have us to be a part of some things in order to serve, and that's it. There are times when it may have absolutely nothing to do with us, our gifts or our talents. There are times when we're to purely learn how to humble ourselves and serve wherever there's a need. So no one in the flesh recognizing you may be the truth and nothing but the truth, but know that God recognizes you. Second, it could be all a part of God's divine plan for your life. So if this is the situation, guess what? Since it's not man's fault, you will have to trust God to use you the way He wills whenever and however He wills.

I only need God is another reason people refuse to submit. God does not feel the same because if He did, He would have never allowed Ephesians 4:11 to be written. It says, "*And **He Himself** gave some to be apostles, some prophets, some evangelists, and some pastors and teachers.*" Why is this? Verse 12 and 13 tells us: "*For the equipping of the saints for the work of ministry, for the edifying of the body of Christ, till we all come to the unity of the faith and of the knowledge of the Son of God, to a perfect man, to the measure of the stature of the fullness of Christ.*"

There may definitely be times in our relationship with God when for different reasons He'll allow us to walk alone with Him. When this happens, we must be assured it's only for a season and not to be mistaken as a permanent situation. We're told from the heart of God in Hebrews 10:24-25 that He desires for us to: *"Consider one another in order to stir up love and good works, **not forsaking the assembling of ourselves together**, as is the manner of some, but exhorting one another, and so much the more as you see the Day approaching."*

Nobody relates to me is the last reason I'd like to point out. I must say and trust me; there is somebody who relates to everybody. This is one of the reasons God allowed there to be so many different kinds of people who serve Him with such an array of different personalities and gifts. In fact, since God created us as such a diverse people of various cultures, languages, experiences, etc., He continuously permits a multitude of different individuals to be raised up for the work of the ministry. Personally, because of the phenomenal benefits I've received as a result of having submitted to different vessels of God in order to grow and learn, I highly encourage every set apart vessel of God to submit.

In closing, I know this may have, been a very sensitive topic for some to think about, but I still pray that in one way or another it has encouraged those of you who are not submitted to do so. When you do, I can guarantee that you will begin to walk out your divine purpose in a greater capacity and do it within the order of God for your life. You will also be positioned to lay hold of all God has for you.

Walk It Out and Focus Questions

> ➢ What should you do if you are not submitted to anyone? First, pray for God's leading, and then actively seek out ministries and/or individuals who can do all of the following: teach from a biblical perspective, exhort, rebuke (correct) you, if needed, and who will at least be aware of what you do for God.
> ➢ When satan chose not to submit to God any longer, what was the consequences of his decision? The answer is found in Isaiah 14:12-17. Please read it.
> ➢ Proverbs 18:1 tells us: *"A man who **isolates** himself seeks his own _____; He rages against all wise judgment."* Please look up this verse to locate the missing word in this passage.

Let's Agree in Prayer: *Lord, if there are any areas within me that have been bruised by leadership and are currently hindering my ability to trust others again, I pray now, Lord, for the strength to forgive so it no longer paralyzes or stifles me from giving as well as being able to receive Your total fullness for my life. In Jesus' name I pray. Amen.*

Chapter 29: Do not Grow Weary in Well Doing

Your Labor Is not in Vain

This chapter is especially dedicated to those who've been faithful and graced by God to sow much of their time, energy, and resources into the lives and visions of others, yet have not been able to see the vision God has placed inside of them and all that He has promised them for their lives come to pass. If this is you, this is God's direct way of letting you know that He knows and cares, so much so, He wouldn't even allow me to finish writing this book without singling you out and intentionally encouraging you. This chapter was also written to remind you of His word which says: *"God is not unjust to forget your work and labor of love which you have shown toward His name, in that you have ministered to the saints, and do minister"* (Hebrews 6:10).

Let me declare this truth to you. Now is not the time for any us to grow weary in well doing because we are right around the corner, if not already exactly where we need to be, to see our breakthrough. Even the word of God encourages us to persevere by saying: *"And we desire that each one of you show the same diligence to the full assurance of hope until the end, **that you do not become sluggish, but imitate those who through faith and patience inherit the promises**"* (Hebrews 6:11-12).

> **Now is not the time for any of us to grow weary in our well doing, because we are right around the corner, if not already exactly where we need to be in order to see our breakthrough.**

Notice how this passage tells us we need both faith and patience in order to lay hold of the promises. Yet, if for some reason you've already become weary if not completely discouraged during your time of waiting, I'd like to encourage you NOT to ignore any feelings of weariness you may have. Weariness, I believe, is a direct sign set up by God for the purpose of getting our attention.

If we stop and take heed of it, I also believe these feelings will help us actually get to our desired destination. Therefore, if you start having feelings of weariness, the best thing you can do for yourself is bring everything to a complete halt regardless of the type of involvement. The sole purpose for doing this is so you can re-focus, spend time with God, and ask Him to help you recognize the root of your weariness.

While many say we should not question God, the bible says if we lack wisdom let us ask God because He gives it liberally without reproach (James 1:5). God wants us to come to Him; therefore, we should ask God questions like, "God is it me? Is it what I'm doing? Is it who or what I'm serving, and if so, what do I need to do to re-adjust?" If you don't take a closer look and ignore your weariness, then I can guarantee you it will resurface at some point. That's, of course, if you don't completely give out first because you can only run injured or on empty for so long.

As a servant of the Lord, trust me; I can understand how you can get to the point where after you've sown your little heart out, you find yourself saying, "I'm not doing anything else for anybody else unless I'm in some way taken care of or at the least made to feel appreciated." However, when feelings like this start to arise in us, that's our first clue we definitely need to get into our "prayer closet" with our heavenly Father. He is the only One who can see our hearts and heal them. Because I've experienced this firsthand, I purposely wrote about weariness hoping that none of us will miss out on our due season, harvest, and breakthrough all because (you name it) has made us weary.

In fact, I'll share one of my own experiences when I grew weary while serving a particular ministry. I noticed toward the end of my assignment that everything in this ministry started to get on my nerves. Then after I was finally able to get alone with God, I realized my weariness was present only because I was no longer graced to do what I had been doing. This meant my time there was up so if I continued to stay, I would've had to do it in my own strength without God's help. Yet, God knew that I in no way wanted to see something He had once used me to be a blessing to turn out to be a nightmare for others or me because I stayed pass my assigned time. Therefore, I chose to be obedient to God so I could exit in the same way I came, as a blessing (a dispenser of good to others).

There are so many things that can contribute to weariness, and I'd like to address a few of them. Let me start by saying if your time is expired as mine was, if it was never God's will for you to have been a part of something, or if you're in a position where you constantly pour out but are not being replenished, weariness can definitely be a consequence. Regardless of the cause of weariness, it must be addressed and not ignored.

I've seen many who've truly had a heart to serve Christ, unfortunately, miss out on some really great opportunities because they grew weary and let it go on for too long unaddressed. When you're weary and it's not addressed, it will start to affect your ability to discern; that will make it very hard for you to even know what is of God and what's not. I believe this is the reason we've all been warned in Proverbs 4:23 to "*Keep our heart with **all** diligence, since out of it spring the issues of life.*"

If you do experience weariness and it appears as if absolutely no good whatsoever can come from it, I'm here to testify if the situation is handled correctly it may actually turn out to be phenomenal for you. When I think back to the times I was weary, every single one of them ended up leading to major breakthroughs in my life. However, this did not happen until I first acknowledged my weariness, and then heeded my God-given instructions.

If by chance you are currently in a state of weariness, please hide this word in your heart; know that whatever you may be feeling or thinking, the seeds you have sown into the lives and visions of others *have not been in vain*. You may not always be able to see the results of your planted seeds, but I can tell you the word of God says: "***You shall reap as long as you do not lose heart***" (Galatians 6:9). Be encouraged!

Walk It Out and Focus Questions

> ➤ Look up the word "weariness" in a thesaurus and identify other signs of weariness and other words that are synonymous with weariness. This will help you to address every form of it on the spot so that it doesn't stay and fester.
> ➤ When serving others, make sure you constantly keep the dream and vision God has given you in view, working on it as much as possible. When you're able to see progress in some things that were once vague, that, within itself, is enough to bring about renewed strength and joy.
> ➤ David is a good biblical example of one who had to go to God during his times of weariness. Please read 1 Samuel 30:1-6 to discover what David did in order to find relief during that time.
> ➤ When you are weary, learn how to strengthen and encourage yourself in the Lord by praying and standing on the word of God. This will help you stay focused on the truth and God's refreshing instead of the lies and sometimes difficult process you are going through.

Let's Agree in Prayer: *Father, please help me to remain steadfast and unmovable in the predestined will and call You have for my life. Please repair all the holes that have been left in me from past hurt, pain, disappointment, and abuse. And instead, let it all be used as the fuel I need in order to stay and complete my course. Lord, please renew me afresh as I give you full permission to go beyond the surface of my life. In Jesus' name I pray. Amen.*

Chapter 30: Don't Believe the Hype

The Grass Is <u>NOT</u> Greener on the Other Side

During your set apart journey with God, whatever you do, please, please, please do not allow yourself to believe the hype portrayed by the lifestyle of non-believers who live contrary to the will of God. You know the hype like "Everything is just oh so lovely." I call it hype because that's all it is. Hype is defined by the Encarta Dictionary as being 1) Something that's greatly exaggerated 2) Somebody or something over publicized 3) A deception or dishonest scheme.

Isn't that interesting?

I'd also like to caution you against allowing yourself to be thrown off by even watching "so called saints," who just live any ol' kind of way, and then act like the way they live is of God. Trust me this can also cause you to be "jacked up," that is, confuse you and get you off of God's ordained path for your life. There really are a lot of folks out there who can put on a great "front" and façade in God. Yet, we can praise God, their fronts will not last. 2 Timothy 2:19 tells us: *"Nevertheless the solid foundation of God stands, having this seal: **The Lord knows those who are His** . . ."*

> **Whatever you do, please do not believe any of the "hype" that's portrayed by the lifestyle of non-believers, who live contrary to the will of God.**

Unquestionably, I understand that trying to stay focused on Christ is not always an easy thing to do especially when you may see folks who have no Godly intentions, whatsoever, receive all the accolades. While there you are, on the other hand, constantly trying to deny your flesh and things of this world in order to please God, but you feel like you're being kept in the background. However, if you feel like I just described, know that your current situation is not permanent. **GOD IS STILL IN CONTROL.** What God is actually allowing you to acquire is something that is eternal and not the brief, short-lived, fleeting treasures of this world. I said brief and fleeting treasures because Matthew 6:19-20 tells us: *"Do not lay up for yourselves treasures on earth, where moth and rust destroy and where thieves break in and steal; but lay up for yourselves treasures in heaven, where neither moth nor rust destroys and where thieves do not break in and steal."*

Don't get me wrong . . . I do admit that seeing all the "bling-bling", ice, platinum, rides, cribs, gluttony in this and that can undeniably be a huge distraction. The temptation of it all can cause any one of us to easily be led astray if we're not extremely cautious. However, we must search out what the word of God says about this.

1 Corinthians 10:13 tells us: *"No temptation has overtaken you except such as is common to man; **but God is faithful**, who will not allow you to be tempted beyond what you are able, **but with the temptation will also make the way of escape**, that you may be able to bear it.*

A part of the escape from the trap of coveting is found in Colossians 3:1-4: "*If then you were raised with Christ, seek those things which are above, where Christ is, sitting at the right hand of God. **Set your mind on things above, not on things on the earth**. For you died, and your life is hidden with Christ in God. When Christ who is our life appears, then you also will appear with Him in **glory**.*"

I must say the God we serve is so awesome because instead of simply allowing us to believe the "hype" and be defeated like He could, He encourages us with His word to stand flat footed in Him by providing us with scriptures like Proverbs 13:21: "*Evil pursues sinners, but to the righteous, good shall be repaid*", Proverbs 12:21 "*No grave trouble will overtake the righteous, But the wicked shall be filled with evil.*"

Further, Proverbs 11:5 says, "*The righteousness of the blameless will direct his way aright, But the wicked will fall by his own wickedness.*" Mind you, these are only a few of hundreds of other scriptures God has given to prevent us from being deceived into thinking that the grass is greener where sinners reside. By no means is it!

Meanwhile, one thing we all have to remember is that if there is no repentance and acceptance of Jesus by non-believers, there will be no salvation. If that happens, everything we see today that glistens and seems glamorous will only have been gained in vain. I'm sure you already know there is no way that any of us can purchase our souls or even peace on this earth for that matter.

Psalm 49:16-17 in the New International Version tells us: "*Do not be overawed when a man grows rich, when the splendor of his house increases; for he will take nothing with him when he dies, his splendor will not descend with him.*"

Jesus gives us wisdom about coveting in Luke 12:15. This is something we all should heed today.

In the Amplified version it reads: "*And He said to them, Guard yourselves and keep free from all covetousness (the immoderate desire for wealth, the greedy longing to have more); for a man's life does not consist in and is not derived from possessing overflowing abundance or that which is over and above his needs.*"

In fact, as a direct way to help encourage you not to believe the hype, I'd like us to take a look at what Malachi 3:13-18 says about both the righteous and wicked, in the Amplified version.

"*Your words have been strong and hard against Me, says the Lord. Yet you say, what have we spoken against You? You have said, it is useless to serve God, and what profit is it if we keep His ordinances and walk gloomily and as if in mourning apparel before the Lord of hosts? And now we consider the proud and arrogant to be happy and favored; evildoers are exalted and prosper; yes, and when they test God, they escape [unpunished]. Then those who feared the Lord talked often one to another; and the Lord listened and heard it, and a book of remembrance was written before Him of those who reverenced and worshipfully feared the Lord and who thought on His name. And they shall be Mine, says the Lord of hosts, in that day when I publicly recognize and openly declare them to be My jewels (My special possession, My peculiar treasure). And I will spare them, as a man spares his own son who serves him. Then shall you return and discern between the righteous and the wicked, between him who serves God and him who does not serve him."*

As we see from the above passage, although it might appear that those who are living "foul" and out of the will of God are "off the hook", in reality they are not! When the appointed time arrives, judgment will arrive also. This is why I intentionally set out to urge you in this chapter to stay focused above all on your eternal reward. By doing so, you can enter through the narrow gate that leads to life instead of the wide spacious gate that leads to destruction. (Matthew 7:13-14)

Walk It Out and Focus Questions

> ➤ As a way to help you stay focused "on the things above and not beneath," I'd like to encourage you to do an in-depth bible study on the benefits you've been given having accepted Jesus as your personal Lord and Savior. After you complete your list, post it somewhere you can see it daily, and review it often so you may receive strength during your time of need.
> ➤ Make a habit of always thanking God for all you have instead of focusing on what you don't have. One way you can do this is by keeping what I'd like to call a "blessing journal". This is something you can write in on a frequent basis recording what God has done and is doing for you. This will help you to acknowledge God and stay focused on Him being your greatest gift ever.
> ➤ Reading Malachi 3:13-18 and Malachi 4:1-3 over and over will help you keep things in the right perspective as it pertains to the outcomes of the godly and the wicked. Truly the wicked will be judged, and the righteous shall be honored.
> ➤ What does Proverbs 11:4 tells us about wealth and righteousness?

Let's Agree in Prayer: *Father, please allow me to receive great insight into all the benefits I've been granted in You so I may clearly know there is absolutely nothing this world or the devil could ever offer to compare to what You've already given me here on earth as well as that which is yet to come once I get to heaven. In Jesus' name I pray. Amen.*

Chapter 31: What if This Was It?

Maximize Your Time

After hearing a Christian artist once say that the reason why he didn't include the name of Jesus much in his music was because he wanted to take his time and work his way up with the whole Christ message. It was impressed upon my heart to ask him, "What if this was it?" Because immediately I thought to myself, "Wow! What if this artist is not given the time he thinks he'll have to do it later?" I mean, what if there's not another chance to share; what if there's not another interview; what if there's not another song, not another opportunity? What if, what if, what if?

In fact, the same question, "What if this was it?" should also be considered and answered by those who've said things like: *"I don't want to be a holy roller because I don't want people to think I can't relate and/or I'm just trying to be different."* Because in some instances, for the individuals who've made comments like that instead of representing Christ to the fullest, not being a holy roller and being different has become their primary focus. Unfortunately, some have been cleverly led astray.

What if the next time we stand before people it becomes our last, what would be heard and or seen?

Truthfully, even I had to come face to face with the "What if this was it?" question because after I heard some time ago of a producer who asked a group of artists before they entered the studio, "If this was your last time to record for Christ what would you say?" That question provoked me to check myself because up until then, I had never even thought about not having the time to do what I needed to do for Christ. I mean seriously, for some odd reason, I just thought since I was a Christian I'd always be guaranteed the time to do whatever I needed to do for Christ whenever *I* wanted to do it.

Later, I realized that my attitude was arrogant especially after reading James 4:14-15, which states: *"Why, you do not even know what will happen tomorrow. What is your life? You are a mist that appears for a little while and then vanishes. Instead, you ought to say, "If it is the Lord's will, we will live and do this or that."*

And so, in essence after having heard that producer's question as well as having read the above passage in the word of God, I was not only convicted but was also challenged to pay greater attention to the true seriousness of what I was saying and doing when given the opportunity to minister. In addition, I became fully aware of the fact that I could only do for the Lord whatever He allowed and willed for me to do, so it would be in my best interest not to take my time here on earth for granted - - - not a single day.

It became obvious to me when the producer asked, the "What if this was it?" question, he took what he did for Christ seriously and wanted to make sure those he worked with were, likewise, going to do the same. I present the same question to all of you who are reading this book because what if the next time we have an opportunity to stand and minister to God's people was our last time? What would be heard and/or seen? Would we be bragging about our rims, our ride, our ice, platinum, loot, clothes, or maybe even our skills in doing whatever it is we do? In other words, would our audience only hear or see us refer to the things of this world which are coming to nothing, or perhaps see us display our flesh which also can do absolutely nothing for them? I hope this question has the same impact on you as it did on me!

Do we really go forth every time we get the opportunity to do so with a high level of awareness of the importance of what we are doing?

If not, we really should re-evaluate our priorities especially since James 4:14 admonishes us that we do not know what will happen tomorrow.

Furthermore, keep in mind that James 4:14 pertains to our lives, but it also relates to the lives of others. You never know the state of others' souls. What I mean by that is when God has been trying to reach out to individuals for quite a while, only He knows whether or not that person has years, months, days, minutes or even seconds, for that matter, to live. This is why it is vitally important that we operate out of the wisdom of God and be ministry-minded instead of *me*, *myself*, and *I* minded.

In fact, as it deals with the timing of one's soul salvation, I can remember years ago wrestling back and forth with God over His desire for me to share a rap I had written at a friend's birthday party. My reason for not wanting to do it was because, quite frankly, God didn't let me know He wanted me to share it until I was actually in the car headed over to the party. So, of course, I was not as prepared as I would have liked to have been, having time to memorize all the lyrics; I didn't want to share it. Not to mention I was also feeling extremely shy and fearful wondering what would happen if my friend didn't want to hear me rap. In short, the outcome of the situation was that God won because before the night was over, I did somehow muster up the strength in God to be obedient to His will and rapped.

Once I finally finished rapping, it was a very awkward situation. However, Lord was I glad I had done so because little did I know I'd never be given the opportunity to do it for him again! I found out a couple of months later, he had been killed in a car accident. Now, I'm sure you can imagine this experience and the lasting imprint it made in my heart and mind. Particularly, it impacted me concerning the true importance of not taking my time or talent for granted but to also not take the lives of others for granted. The significance of always being obedient to the Lord's leading in all things was made even clearer to me.

Having shared that particular experience, I hope it helped to emphasize the true need for us to maximize the time we've been given. So, if you haven't already started to give God your best for His best, prayerfully you will begin to do so while you've been granted the grace, time, energy, and mercy needed to do just that.

Walk It Out and Focus Questions

➤ Set out to truly make your life count in every opportunity you have to be present before God's people. In addition, ask yourself these questions every time you walk away from being involved in an event: *"What did the people really receive? Did they receive more of me and my flesh than of God and His Son?"* If your answer is more of you, then please know there needs to be a shift so that God can be the focus.

➤ Since God has allotted all of us a certain number of days while here on this earth, perhaps our prayer should become Psalm 90:12 which reads: "So teach us to number our days that we may gain a heart of wisdom."

➤ In John 4:31-34, the disciples noticed that Jesus had not eaten anything in a long while, and they urged Him saying, "Rabbi, eat." But He said to them, "I have food to eat of which you do not know." Therefore the disciples said to one another, "Has anyone brought Him anything to eat?" And in verse 34 Jesus responded to them by saying, "My food is to do the will of Him who sent Me, and to finish His work." Here, we see Jesus had more of a desire to do the will of God than even His own natural need for food. Reflect on verse 34, and ask yourself if you also have the same intense desire as Jesus had to serve God? If not, this should certainly become your aim, so you can be able to know without a doubt that there is purposeful substance to all you do.

Let's Agree in Prayer: *Lord, please help me to do all I do for You as if I will never be given another chance to do so, and that as a result, I may give my all to whatever is at hand and be used in the exact way You'd have me to be. Help me to always remember that time is of the essence. In Jesus' name I pray. Amen.*

A Word of Exit

The Journey

If you have read this book in its entirety, it is evident to me but most importantly to God, that you truly do have a heart's desire to use your gifts and talents in the "set apart way". Hopefully, you have discovered that the set apart way is doing things in a way that only God is glorified. I'd personally like to commend you for dedicating yourself to finding out what God's will is for you through this book.

There is one more thing I'd like to make you aware of, and that is this: walking and living out the set apart way is truly a lifetime journey. I say that because in order for you to stay on the straight and narrow path God has ordained for you, you will constantly have to say "no" to your flesh, "no" to the world, and "no" to the devil, who is all too eager to lead you astray. However, as long as you continue to do as you've done with this book, placing yourself in an environment to receive continued strength and wisdom for your journey, you will be victorious, as Jesus was, over all the works of the devil.

As a matter of fact, to help you do that, I'd like to invite you to make another investment into your spiritual walk with Christ by joining the SACA Mentorship Program. This is a mentorship program that has been specifically designed with you, a creative artist, in mind. So definitely take advantage of it.

To find out more about this program, go to Setapartinternationalministries.org or simply read the next page for further information.

May the Lord, our God, continue to establish the work of your hands for His glory! In Jesus' name I pray. Amen.

Grateful to serve,

Sepia

SACA MENTORSHIP PROGRAM
We welcome you to join today!

If you have just finished reading this book, "The Set Apart Way for Christ-Centered Creative Artists," you've already completed half of the program requirements in order to become a SACA member. With just a few more steps, you will be a full member. What is a SACA member, and how will you benefit from it? Please find out below!

Set Apart International Ministries
Presents

God is calling all of His creative artists to a higher standard in Him. The real question is, "Will we, individually as well as collectively, answer the call?" If so, we welcome you to become a part of the Set Apart Creative Artist (SACA) Mentorship Program. This is a program dedicated to helping you answer the "set apart call" by encouraging you to be a set apart vessel for God's use. We encourage you to use your gifts and talents for His glory.

What we provide:

- **Mentorship** - By giving you practical insight on different ways you can go about giving God the glory while using your gifts and talents.
- **Support and encouragement** - By either introducing you to the Set Apart Lifestyle or continuing to encourage you to live out the Set Apart Lifestyle for your entire journey toward purpose and destiny.
- **Fellowship** - By introducing you to other set apart creative artists, who have the same passion as you do.
- **Accountability** - By periodically coming into direct contact with you via calls, emails, letters, etc. in order to encourage you and assist in holding you accountable.
- **Prayer** - We are committed to fast as well as continually pray on your behalf while you are out in the trenches fulfilling the work of the ministry

This Ministry is specifically designed to **serve you** so in return you may continue to be equipped and encouraged in a greater way to **serve others**.

SIGN UP TODAY!

Out of our desire to the see the Body of Christ edified and God glorified as He deserves, this mentorship program will only cost you your time and the cost of purchasing two required books for the program. Although there are no additional monetary costs associated with this program, we ask each artist to complete the following requirements in order to become a member:

Requirements to become a SACA member are as follows:

- ✓ **Complete the Set Apart Creative Artist Profile.** This is where you're asked questions like your name, address, what it is you do for the Lord while using your gifts and talents, email address, prayer request, etc. We ask this of you because again we are here to serve you, and it helps us to know those who we are serving and their specific needs.

- ✓ **Purchase required reading material for the program.** This book is the first reading assignment. *The Set Apart Way for Christ-Centered Creative Artists Bible Study Workbook* is also required." Because this mentor program was birthed through the writing of these books, we ask each artist to obtain a copy of each and read them.

- ✓ **Write a short essay after each chapter** while reading *The Set Apart Way for Christ-Centered Creative Artists*. For each essay, we only ask that you explain what meant the most to you from the chapter or offered you the greatest challenge, inspired or confirmed what you already knew. After the essays have been written, you can e-mail or mail them back to the ministry. *Note*: You can send in the essays one at a time or all together. It's your choice.

- ✓ **Answer all questions in *The Set Apart Way for Christ-Centered Creative Artists Bible Study Workbook*.** This workbook has been specifically designed to take you into a deeper study by directing you to the word of God highlighting different topics that were mentioned in *The Set Apart Way for Christ-Centered Creative Artists*. **Your answers to the questions from the workbook do _not_ have to be turned in for review.** They are to be kept for your personal study.

A WHOLE YEAR TO COMPLETE

Realizing that most of us have busy schedules, we ask that both the essays and questions to the workbook are completed within a year's time after you begin.

Upon completion of the above requirements, you will be a SACA Member / Graduate and will receive the following:

- ▪ A **Personalized Certificate** signed by the founder of Set Apart International Ministries congratulating you on completing the mentorship program.

- **Name entered into a drawing to receive a $200** check to go toward your personal endeavors for the Kingdom of God. (Drawings held yearly)

- **Name listed on our website** as a SACA Member / Graduate and possibly your contact information as long as whatever you do for the Lord lines up with our vision.

- **Access to Quarterly messages** to encourage your set apart walk with the Lord from the founder. (Beginning soon)

IF INTERESTED IN JOINING IT IS EASY TO GET STARTED.

ALL YOU HAVE TO DO IS THE FOLLOWING:

1. Log on to Setapartinternationalministries.org.

2. Click on the SACA (Set Apart Creative Artists) tab.

3. Scroll down and click on the red <u>SIGN UP TODAY</u> link.

4. Fill out the form.

5. Submit the form once all information required is completed.

It's that easy!

- You can start sending in your essays as soon as you are ready.
- Purchase the corresponding Bible Study Workbook from our website to answer the questions.

If you have any questions about the mentorship program, please do not hesitate to contact us at **info@setapartinternationalministries.org**.

We thank you in advance for joining and look forward to serving you in the future!

Invitation

If by chance you have not accepted Jesus Christ as your personal Lord and Savior, I must tell you because I have done so, it has been **the greatest, life-impacting thing** I have ever done in my life. For Jesus has without a shadow of a doubt changed everything about me for the better, and I am ever so grateful to God for Him allowing me to have come into relationship with His Son, who is "the way, the truth, and the life" (John 14:6). And so, if you also are interested in accepting Jesus as your personal Lord and Savior, God's word tells us all we have to do is this: "confess with your mouth the Lord Jesus and believe in your heart that God has raised Him from the dead, and you will be saved for with the heart one believes unto righteousness, and with the mouth confession is made unto salvation" (Romans 10:9-10). After you make this confession ask God to lead you to a bible believing church where you can attend, so your faith in Jesus Christ can continue to grow. Romans 10:17 tells us: "So then faith comes by hearing, and hearing by the word of God."

About the Author

Sepia Gladden, affectionately known by many as "Sista Sepia." is a creative artist who ministers through spoken word, poetry, and gospel rap. She is also a radio host, abstinence instructor, inspirational speaker and minister of the gospel of Jesus Christ.

Sepia has a strong passion to see God be given the glory He deserves in the lives of believers and creative artists. She is particularly endeavoring to reach those who've already made or would like some guidance in making the decision to use their gifts and talents for His glory. Sepia does this by encouraging all to live out the "set apart" lifestyle.

Currently, Sepia, along with her husband, Apostle Anthony Gladden, are the founders of Set Apart International Ministries, a ministry specifically designed to lift Jesus and encourage the Set Apart lifestyle in the lives of believers for God's glory. Set Apart International Ministries not only ministers to the Body of Christ as a whole but specifically to creative artists around the world by way of the SACA Mentorship Program. You can learn more about the ministry by going to her website, **www.Setapartinternationalministries.org**.

For more information about Sepia's books or to give a testimony about how God used this book as a blessing in your life, please email Sepia at: info@setapartinternationalministries.org

To arrange speaking or ministry engagements, please contact:

info@setapartinternationalministries.org